# CITIZENVILLE

HOW TO TAKE
THE
TOWN SQUARE
DIGITAL
AND
REINVENT
GOVERNMENT

## GAVIN NEWSOM
WITH LISA DICKEY

PENGUIN BOOKS

PENGUIN BOOKS
Published by the Penguin Group
Penguin Group (USA) LLC
375 Hudson Street
New York, New York 10014

USA | Canada | UK | Ireland | Australia | New Zealand | India | South Africa | China
penguin.com
A Penguin Random House Company

First published in the United States of America by The Penguin Press,
a member of Penguin Group (USA) Inc., 2013
Published in Penguin Books 2014

THE LIBRARY OF CONGRESS HAS CATALOGED THE HARDCOVER EDITION AS FOLLOWS:
Newsom, Gavin Christopher.
Citizenville : how to take the town square digital and reinvent government /
Gavin Newsom with Lisa Dickey.
pages cm
Includes index.
ISBN 978-1-59420-472-2 (hc.)
ISBN 978-0-14-312447-4 (pbk.)
1. Internet in public administration—United States.  2. Democracy—United States.
3. Political participation—United States.  I. Dickey, Lisa.  II. Title.
JF1525.A8N497 2013
352.3'802854678—dc23
2012039619

Printed in the United States of America
1  3  5  7  9  10  8  6  4  2

DESIGNED BY STEPHANIE HUNTWORK

FOR MY WIFE, JEN; MY CHILDREN,
MONTANA AND HUNTER; MY SISTER, HILARY;
MY FATHER, BILL; AND MY MOTHER, TESSA

*As citizens of this democracy, you are the rulers and the ruled,*
*the law-givers and the law-abiding, the beginning and the end.*
—ADLAI STEVENSON

*The government is us; we are the*
*government, you and I.*
——THEODORE ROOSEVELT

# CONTENTS

# INTRODUCTION

THIS BOOK STARTED WITH A QUESTION. Over the past several years, I've found myself wondering: Why is it that people are more engaged than ever with each other—through Twitter, Pinterest, Facebook, text messaging—but less engaged with their government?

Millions of Americans can find hours every day to tweet, text, blog, post reviews, and play games with each other on social-networking sites. Yet in 2011 when our second-largest city, Los Angeles, held an election on crucial initiatives dealing with education and the environment, only 12 percent of registered voters found time to cast a ballot. And the low turnout was so unremarkable, so par for the course, that hardly anyone even noticed or commented on it.

Where was the disconnect coming from? And what could we do to fix it?

Then I realized something else. It wasn't just that people weren't engaging with their government. Elected officials weren't bothering to engage with the people, either—that is, of course, until campaign time. I don't know about you, but I never feel so needed and loved as during the months leading up to an election, when I'm suddenly bombarded with e-mails, calls, and pleas for donations. I'm an elected official myself and find it annoying, so I can only imagine that everyone else finds it even more so.

Politicians love to use social media—but only for getting people involved in campaigns or getting into their wallets. We build fancy Web sites; we ramp up our tweeting and texting and engaging and mashing up; we host online town halls. And then, once we get elected, we just shut all that off and go away—until the next campaign season rolls around. No wonder people feel disconnected.

Campaigns—great campaigns—become movements. They create enthusiasm and buy-in and connection. JFK with his "We can do better," Reagan with "Morning in America," Obama with "Yes we can" . . . A great campaign is a spirited, almost spiritual thing. It makes you want to do more. But nowadays, all that disappears the minute the election is over. During the campaign, we convince people to open themselves up—they let themselves hope, they let themselves believe, they let their guard down. And then we get into office and we hold a couple of Twitter town halls where we answer questions for one hour in 140-character responses. "Well, John, I appreciate your question." That's not civic engagement. It's merely cosmetic.

Politicians often say, "This is what the American people want," but the truth is, most of them have no idea what people want. Average citizens have very few ways to make their voices heard in government, and the ones they do have are archaic: calling their representatives, sending a letter or e-mail, and voting every once in a while. What "the American people" want is most often determined by random polls, which usually means the opinions of people who happen to answer their landline phones, as cell-phone polling is still the exception rather than the rule.

Government right now is functioning on the cutting edge—of 1973. In the private sector and in our personal lives, absolutely everything has changed over the last decade. In government very little has. For the first time in history, anyone with a smartphone can have all the world's information literally in the palm of his or her hand. People have embraced that blessing with passion, desire, and innovation, creating apps, games, tools, and Web sites that improve their daily lives. But government has held it at arm's length while our problems have gotten worse.

So how do we fix this problem? How can we bridge this gap between technology and government?

To find out, I decided to talk to people at the core of the issue: the technologists, politicians, thinkers, and innovators whose work is changing not only the way we communicate, but also the way we live. Over the last eighteen months, I've interviewed dozens of people all over the United States—people like Yelp cofounder Jeremy Stoppelman, former president Bill Clinton, new-media mogul Arianna Huffington, X Prize founder Peter Diamandis, Twitter cofounder Evan Williams, and the legendary innovator Stewart Brand, among many others.

I asked all of them how we can use the amazing new tools of technology to get people excited about and engaged in government again and what they saw as the future of citizen participation in this hyperconnected age. Their answers—often surprising and always enlightening—form the backbone of this book.

Each of these people brought something unique to the table, but taken as a whole, their thoughts added up to one overarching message: The revolution is happening now, and the world is changing too quickly for government to respond with tiny, incremental changes. It is time to radically rethink the relationship between citizens and government.

# VENDING MACHINE VERSUS CLOUD

In his 2008 book, *The Next Government of the United States*, public policy expert Donald Kettl wrote that the government is like a vending machine. You put in money, and you get out goods and services.

It's a good analogy, true to the way our government has traditionally worked. But then Tim O'Reilly, a brilliant Web 2.0 guy and open-source software pioneer, took it a step further. In a 2009 essay on *TechCrunch*, Tim wrote:

> Too often, we think of government as a kind of vending machine. We put in our taxes, and get out services: roads, bridges, hospitals, fire brigades, police protection. . . . And when the vending machine doesn't give us what we want, we protest. Our idea of citizen engagement has somehow been reduced to shaking the vending machine.

This is the perfect analogy. Is there any more frustrating pursuit than shaking a vending machine? Your money has disappeared, you didn't get the thing you want, and even if you do manage to shake something loose, you still can't change the fundamental fact that someone else decided what you could buy from that machine in the first place. You're pretty much powerless throughout the entire process, except for that last resort of shaking the machine in anger and frustration.

In the past few years, people have been shaking that vending machine all around the world. The Arab Spring, the Occupy movement, the Tea Party conventions, students protesting tuition hikes—these are examples of people shaking the machine because there's no other way to get those in power to listen. Something's obviously broken when the only way people know how to get their government's attention is by camping in downtown squares, marching and protesting, screaming at those in charge.

So what should we do? The predictable answer would be "Fix the vending machine!" But the better answer is to throw it out altogether. If we're going to bring government into the twenty-first century, we have to start by completely rethinking what government really is.

A vending machine is a box with finite capacity; you can put in or take out a limited number of things, and you have to be physically near it to make it work. The same is true of computers. Right now, most of us keep our information on hard drives, which means it's accessible only when we're physically sitting next to our computers.

But cloud computing, in which our information is stored on remote servers—such as Gmail for our e-mail, Flickr for our photos, and Google Docs for our files—makes information accessible anywhere, anytime, on any device. It's about being able to simply drive the car without having to build and maintain it. The cloud is an on-demand resource, freeing us from the constraints of place, letting us share, communicate, and connect more easily than ever before.

Why is this important? Because the future is about information—being able to access it, manipulate it, learn from it, improve our lives with it. And the cloud's sole purpose is to give us information whenever, wherever we need it. The cloud is ubiquity, access, sharing, collaboration, connection. It works for you.

That is how our twenty-first-century government must operate. As the futurist and author Peter Schwartz says, "[The cloud] enables the enterprise to organize itself in a distributed fashion, without central power, to deliver and collaborate in ways that you couldn't before." In other words, it gives power to the people, which is the first crucial step in moving away from the top-down, bureaucratic, hierarchical government that's choking our democracy today. Understanding this concept is central to understanding how the government must change and what it must become.

## THE COLLABORATION STAGE

With the explosion of social networking, smartphones, and apps, we have the tools available right now, in our hands, to transform government. We just have to have the courage to use them.

The early World Wide Web—Web 1.0—was all about information. It was a way for people to find pieces of data more easily than ever before. But Web 2.0 is something different. It's about collaboration rather than information. It's about networking, sharing, organizing, reaching out to one another.

Our government today is still in 1.0 mode. You can go to SF311.org and get information about trash pickup, road work, streetlight repair. You can go to the Web sites of different government departments and download documents, applications, reports. But we haven't yet reached Government 2.0—the collaboration stage, in which businesses and social networks are operating today. That's the stage we have to get to in order to innovate our way out of this mess: We have to engage the collective wisdom of people outside of government, rather than just relying, as we always have, on those who work within the monolith.

Examples of how to do this abound in the private sector. Open-source software made it possible for thousands of people to pool their skills and create the popular Firefox browser. An open application programming interface, or API, made it possible for many more to create iPhone apps, in the process spurring revenue growth and creating an entire industry of cool, fun, and useful tools. The controversial, untested, and crazy-sounding notion of opening up an online encyclopedia to thousands of volunteer writer-editors resulted in Wikipedia, now the sixth-most-visited site on the Web.

None of these ventures would exist in a closed, noncollaborative system. They are the wave of the future—a future that's about participation, empowerment, feedback loops, and organically created communities. It's not about elites taking charge, controlling the system, and telling us what's good for us. Through technology, we will learn how to engage millions of people with talent and wisdom to solve our problems.

As the tech journalist Greg Ferenstein has noted, "One way for government 2.0 to be really, really helpful is to make the public useful to their representatives." Government has to allow people to find solutions it can't find on its own. Yet this kind of bottom-up, two-way, nonhierarchical structure is completely antithetical to the way government currently runs. So we have to start with the most basic but most important step. We have to learn to "think different."

## THINKING DIFFERENT

Wim Elfrink, executive vice president and chief globalization officer for Cisco Systems, is a man who makes his living thinking outside the box. He spent years working in Bangalore, India, developing the concept of Smart+Connected Communities—Cicso's trademark term for twenty-first-century cities where technology will be as seamlessly integrated as electricity. I spoke with Elfrink about the need for reinventing American governance, and he told me his own theories about how to do it.

"We are prisoners of our own experiences," he said, and gave me an example. "In India, I was involved in rural villages where we gave every small house a tap, for water. After four weeks, we learned that everyone always left the tap open." These rural Indians didn't understand that they were wasting water—on the contrary, they thought they were keeping it fresh. "These were illiterate people," said Elfrink. "[To them], water has to stream. If water stops, it's not healthy." It's extremely difficult for poor Indians to conceive of a new reality—that stopping a water flow is a good thing—when the opposite has always been true.

Similarly, when the flow of information has always been one way—from government to people, from elites to the middle class, from professor to student, from media to consumers—it's almost impossible for people to conceive of its being any other way. But technology has opened up a two-way stream, and it's here to stay whether we like it or not.

I had my own epiphany about this in 2005, during my first term as mayor of San Francisco. I had gone to Davos for the annual World Economic Forum meetings, and the first big group discussion we had was with representatives of an organization called AmericaSpeaks. They told us about a new technology—handheld devices that allow people to quietly vote on their priorities rather than having to travel to city meetings and strive to argue the loudest for their positions. They could sit in their seats, even at home, and express their opinions through this device, which gave each person's response equal value.

I loved the idea, and asked the woman demonstrating it if it had ever been used for budgeting. "Great idea," she said. So the next year, for San Francisco's budgeting process, we didn't hold our usual contentious town halls where special interests packed the room and people had to fight to be heard. Instead, we held three town-hall meetings dubbed SF Listens, providing these devices for people who wanted a say. The result was a more representative, less special-interest-heavy budget. We called it the People's Budget.

As mayor, that was the first time I realized that technology was about more than making our government Web sites better. This tool enabled us to engage the public more directly and bypass the screamers, who always took so much more attention than they deserved. We used those devices for budgeting several times during my terms as mayor, and by my last year in office, we had thousands of participants and a wave of positive public engagement.

All this was possible because a new device helped me see a different way of doing something we'd been doing the same way for years. What other improvements can we make, if only we open our eyes to the fantastic array of new technologies springing up around us?

## CITIZENVILLE

As I delved deeper into new technologies, a few themes kept popping up: the ubiquity of social media, the changing expectations of a new generation of tech-savvy Americans, the popularity of games and competitions, and the willingness of people to spend time and money on these new pursuits. If we're to have any hope of modernizing government—of bringing it fully into the age of technology—we must embrace all these trends.

FarmVille, created by the gaming company Zynga, embodies all these trends. It's a social game, played online with friends, in which players spend hours maintaining their virtual farms. Players can interact by visiting each other's farms and giving each other gifts, and they can compete to see who harvests the most crops. People spend untold hours playing this game, building their farms and caring for their crops—it's a virtual community with stronger social ties than many real-life communities.

Shauna Robertson, cofounder of the Crowdrise fund-raising and social-networking site, asked me why we couldn't transfer the principles of FarmVille to civic engagement. "Why can't I take ownership of my little area of California and say, 'This is what I want to do—I want to build my schools here'?" Or fix the potholes or landscape the traffic medians? In other words, instead of taking care of a fictional farm, why can't we create a game in which you take care of your actual neighborhood or your town?

We could combine the fun of a game with the social good of solving real problems. Here's one way it could work: Let's say you live in a neighborhood of twenty blocks. If four people there want to play the game—let's call it Citizenville—you can divide the neighborhood into four areas delineated by an interactive map on the Citizenville Web site. Each player takes responsibility for his or her area, and if others living there decide they want to play too, they can either join forces and create a team or subdivide into even smaller areas.

The way to "win" Citizenville is to amass points by doing real-life good. If a player contacts the city to report a pothole and get it fixed, he gets one hundred points. If another player organizes a community cleanup in the local park, she gets two hundred points. If another player landscapes the median on his street, that's three hundred points. Whenever people make a real-life improvement, they report it to the Citizenville Web site, which has a continuously updating scoreboard.

Just as in games like FarmVille, players are spending time improving their areas, competing with each other, and having fun doing so. But the difference is, rather than taking pride in a completely virtual world, the players in Citizenville can walk right out their front doors and see the difference they've made.

The more I thought about it, the more Citizenville came to feel like a kind of shorthand for how the government needs to adapt to this new technological age. Citizenville is more than just a game; it's a new way of thinking about the relationship between people and their government. It's a world in which the old one-way, top-down, bureaucratic, pre-Internet hierarchy is replaced by a truly democratic, bottom-up, social civic engagement. Citizenville is the true implementation of Government 2.0, where the solutions are, increasingly, in our own hands.

## CONNECTING PEOPLE AND GOVERNMENT: FIVE THEMES

In doing research for this book, I've talked with people from many walks of life—including politicians, programmers, researchers, technologists, entrepreneurs, authors, venture capitalists, and students—asking them what we need to do to fix government. The answers have fallen all across the spectrum, but five themes kept coming up again and again. On the face of it, they're simple and straightforward and even seem rather obvious. Taken together, they represent a way to solve numerous problems afflicting us today.

First, government has to be absolutely transparent—every agency, across the board, with exceptions only to protect public safety or personal privacy. We must open up our vast stores of data, make them available to ordinary people, and make sure they are standardized and easy to use.

Second, we must encourage people to use that data to create useful apps, devices, tools—anything they want. We must make it possible for them to build these things easily, to share them, and even to make money on them. It's only through crowdsourcing, feedback loops, and collective wisdom that we can harness the amazing power of the technological revolution. Government can't do it alone.

Third, we must learn to engage people on their own terms. In a world where games, social networking, and 140-character updates are what capture people's attention, we need to integrate those things into government communication. We need to acknowledge that for a whole generation of Americans under the age of thirty, their reality is nothing like the reality the over-thirties grew up with. Under-thirties are, to use terms coined by writer Marc Pensky in 2001, "digital natives," as opposed to "digital immigrants" who learned how to use technology later in life.

Fourth, we need to allow people to bypass government. We must encourage them to take matters into their own hands, to look to themselves for solving problems rather than asking the government to do things for them. New technology is making this more feasible than ever. We have to accept the fact that top-down hierarchy is no longer working and it won't ever work again.

Fifth, we must inject a more innovative, entrepreneurial mind-set into government. In a world where teenagers at home in their bedrooms can create their own music videos, movies, YouTube sensations, interactive maps, mash-ups, and even entire companies, we simply cannot have a government that relies on bureaucracy and maintaining the status quo. The notion that government needs to be more entrepreneurial is not new. But what *is* new is the arrival of technologies that will make this transition easier than at any time in history.

That's how we can reconnect Americans to their government. And the time to start is now.

# ONE

# How Did We Get Here?

WHILE I WAS MAYOR OF SAN FRANCISCO, one afternoon the president of Estonia, Toomas Hendrik Ilves, came by to see me. I didn't get too many visits from heads of state, so this was an occasion. It was just a social call, but I was eager to tell him about all the new, exciting things we had going on in the city.

"What kind of new things?" he asked.

"Well," I said, "we've got all kinds of tech initiatives happening. We're right next door to Silicon Valley, of course, so technology is our friend. For example, I've got three different vendors working on a project right now that would allow people to pay for parking meters with their cell phones." I leaned back in my chair, waiting for his reaction.

He just looked at me blankly. Had I spoken too fast? His English was perfect, as he'd actually grown up in the United States, but he didn't appear to have caught what I'd said.

Finally, he spoke. "We have been doing that for years now," he said. "You can pay for any parking meter in Estonia with a cell phone. You can also pay parking tickets, property taxes—any kind of fee to the government, really."

Now I was the one staring blankly. "Do you have free wi-fi, too?" I asked.

"Yes," he said. "Also for several years now."

Talk about a wake-up call. Americans tend to think of San Francisco as Tomorrowland, on the cutting edge of technology in government, but in fact, we were years behind. I had spent months trying to secure free citywide wi-fi in San Francisco, but the deal had finally been killed by a combination of brutal partisan politics and pushback from existing Internet service providers. And our effort to upgrade parking meters, like any government initiative that requires an outside contractor, was bogged down in procurement issues. Any step toward the future usually ran smack into the obstacles of political and legacy issues.

But Estonia—or E-stonia, as it has been dubbed—was way ahead. A 2009 Public Radio International report helped to explain why:

> Mobile phones in Estonia are in much higher use than landlines. . . . When Estonia came out of the Soviet Union in 1991, there were very few landlines in the country. As the country itself developed in parallel with mobile phone technology, more and more people have mobile phones. Some people have two, sometimes three cell phones.

> In fact, there are nearly two cell phones for every resident of Estonia, giving it a nearly 200 percent penetration rate—one of the highest in the world.

> As a result, people in Estonia are used to using their mobile phones to do everyday things that in the US or in Europe, we would never even think of doing. For example, it's very common in Estonia to pay for your parking meter with your cell phone. You just take out your phone, type in a little code, you send money directly, electronically from your bank account to that parking meter—not a problem.

We clearly had a long way to go to catch up—and a rough road to get there. Government initiatives in the United States, whether local, state, or federal, get bogged down in a thousand different ways. Legacy companies, such as cable providers, fight against new technologies that would undercut their business. Special interests flood the system with cash and block initiatives they don't like. And the civil service, the system under which millions of nonmilitary government employees work, is in many ways stuck in an antiquated mind-set—one that does not provide for flexibility and often rewards longevity over innovation and creativity.

As a newly independent country, Estonia could simply skirt many of these problems. But in America, they're deeply entrenched. "We treat government in this very twentieth-century way," says Peter Hirshberg, a Silicon Valley entrepreneur who blogs about the intersection of technology and business. "There's no dialogue. You could vote, you could complain, you could pay taxes, but then you'd start running out of ways of interacting with the government." On the other hand, "Social media opens up so many gestures. When blogging started, the gestures of social media were you could blog or not. Well, today, you can 'like,' 'location,' 'friend'—there are so many different ways of telegraphing an engagement. So we're opening up lots and lots of different ways of telegraphing engagement with cities. Not that cities are taking full advantage of it—yet. "There's a whole vocabulary of how you engage that's just being learned," Hirshberg told me, "but not yet heralded."

# BUREAUCRACY WANTS TO STOP INNOVATION

Any big entity—not just government—is resistant to change. Go into any large company and announce to the employees that you're switching everyone to a different e-mail system. You won't be met with cheers. Whenever cities are forced to add a new area code to local phone numbers, people act as if their basic human rights have been violated. No one likes having to learn something new, even if it's a relatively simple thing.

But the very nature of government throws another wrench into the works. Because of the vast network of rules, regulations, and laws that apply to virtually everything in government service, people aren't sure what they're *allowed* to do, much less what they're *supposed* to do. Then you get IT (information technology) department people who are paranoid about introducing anything new. Allow open social networking? Switch to cloud computing? That's a bit risky, isn't it? Better to just do things the way we've always done them. Better safe than sorry.

Resisting new technology is the government's default position. Joe Trippi, the guru behind Howard Dean's groundbreaking online presidential campaign in 2004, told me about a lawsuit in California that perfectly illustrates the point. A company in Silicon Valley created a way to sign petitions electronically, but a state official refused to recognize them. Even in the age of DocuSign, when people routinely sign loan papers via e-mail, the official decided that these electronic signatures didn't count. So the petitioners filed suit.

The action led naturally to the question what is a signature, anyway? A signature produced by an autograph machine, which exactly mimics a person's handwriting in ink, is considered legitimate. But what if, instead of physically pushing a button to activate that machine, you could activate it by e-mail? Would that signature still be legal? If so, how is that any different from an e-signature? Will the government pass a law saying there must be physical contact between person, pen, and paper in order to make a signature valid?

It sounds pretty silly when you drill down like that, but to Trippi it's a troubling sign of a larger problem. "Bureaucracy wants to stop innovation," he said, "even stuff that makes improvements in how we do things." Bureaucracy—e.g., government—is slow to adapt at best. At worst, it's openly hostile to change.

The e-signature example is relatively benign. But some other examples involve matters of life and death. The Federal Communications Commission (FCC) has been trying for years to enable people to send text messages to 911, an initiative called NG9-1-1 (NG for next generation). The reason is obvious—there are occasionally times when people are under threat and need to contact emergency services silently. As FCC Chairman Julius Genachowski said in a 2011 speech:

Today, if a mobile phone user attempts to send even a simple text to 9-1-1, it goes nowhere. That's what happened to the students at Virginia Tech who texted 9-1-1 during the terrible shooting several years ago. A tragedy during the 1990s—the carjacking and murder of Jennifer Koon in New York—was significant in spurring the initial focus on NG9-1-1, and is worth recalling. During the incident, Jennifer Koon was able to call 9-1-1 from her car phone but couldn't speak for fear of alerting her attacker. The [9-1-1 call center] kept the line open in the hopes the caller would say something, but she never did and was found dead two hours later. The ability to text 9-1-1 might have saved her life.

The story of Jennifer Koon is unspeakably tragic. But what makes it even worse is the fact that in 2011—a full *eighteen years* after Jennifer's death in 1993—the FCC still hadn't succeeded in implementing NG9-1-1. Eighteen years is a long time, but in the world of technology, it's an eternity. How can the government take so long when people's lives potentially hang in the balance? Why does it move so slowly?

## A HISTORY OF TECHNOPHOBIA

The government's delay in implementing new technologies is a big problem, but it's not a new one. The sad truth is that the history of government is a history of technophobia. Sixty years ago, as President Roosevelt was delivering his fireside chats by radio, Congress was passing laws attempting to keep microphones off the congressional floor. Today, as Americans are sharing and connecting more than ever— photos, music, personal information, location data—we've had to force our government agencies to open up their treasure troves of data. Fear and inertia rule the day.

Matt Lira, the director of new media for Representative Eric Cantor, is one of a handful of people on the cutting edge of technology in government, and he's done a lot of thinking about how we got to this point.

"If you go back and watch fifties congressional hearings, they're terrible," he told me. "They're made for radio, but then they just stuck a TV camera in there. . . . It's embarrassingly bad TV. And when color TV came, the charts were still in gray because of black and white TV." It took years for Congress to adapt, Lira says, but the institution finally caught up. "In modern-day hearings," he says, "you have a feed package, stage lights. It's good television." And just imagine—it only took us six decades to get here.

Watching those old hearings—clear historical evidence of our government's resistance to change—might discourage anyone. Yet Lira says they give him faith in progress. "It's inevitable that we'll make this transformation in the future," he says. "One day, we'll look back and say, 'I can't believe we didn't have the Twitter Wall then!' Or whatever technology has become ubiquitous. We're still at the very beginning of this stuff on both sides of the aisle."

Lira is right about that—we are still at the beginning. But if we're honest, nobody really has any idea where we're going—which is part of the problem. New, exciting technologies come along all the time, but it's hard to know which ones will stick and which will flame out.

In 2011, *New York Times* columnist and author Thomas Friedman famously summed this up, referring to the technological changes that followed publication of his 2005 bestseller *The World Is Flat*:

> When I wrote *The World Is Flat*, Facebook did not exist, Twitter was a sound, the Cloud was in the sky, 4G was a parking space, applications were what you sent to college, LinkedIn was a prison, and for most people, Skype was a typo. All of that changed in just the last six years.

Today, anyone who doesn't know what these things are or how to use them has fallen behind. But in 2005, they were fledgling ideas among thousands of other fledgling ideas. As we've seen time and again, not everything that looks like the next big thing actually makes it there—just ask MySpace, Buzz, or Friendster. New technologies fail much more often than they succeed. Yet you can't swipe through articles on your iPad without seeing dozens of breathless stories of this or that new technology that will supposedly change the world.

When Howard Dean broke the mold in 2004 with his grassroots Internet campaign, the move was heralded as the beginning of a new era. But looking back now, it's amazing how little that era resembles the one we're in now. As Joe Trippi and I talked, he rattled off some numbers:

> On the day the campaign ended, there were 1.4 million blogs in the world. On the day Obama announced, there were 77 million blogs. Facebook was on one college campus in 2004 at the end of the Dean campaign. By 2008, it had a couple hundred million users. . . . Since 2008, the network continues to get more connected. Bandwidth is bigger. . . . But government seems to be the last place that's taking advantage of any of it.

The truth is, not everyone is an early adopter. And it's hard enough to embrace new technologies even when you're sure they'll be around for a while. So how can we expect our big, slow-moving government to be on the front lines of innovation?—especially when the landscape of that innovation is littered with the corpses of so many "next big things."

## A FLEET OF WRIGHT FLYERS

Moving into the twenty-first century might not be so hard if our government weren't mired in a twentieth-century bureaucratic model.

Our basic government structures haven't changed in decades, and the cracks are showing. As former Republican Senate staffer Mike Lofgren has said, "Trying to govern a complex society of 310 million people via a museum piece like the Senate is like trying to operate an airline whose fleet consists of Wright Flyers."

President Obama referred to this problem in his 2011 State of the Union address:

> We can't win the future with a government of the past. We live and do business in the Information Age, but the last major reorganization of the government happened in the age of black-and-white TV. There are 12 different agencies that deal with exports. There are at least five different agencies that deal with housing policy. Then there's my favorite example: the Interior Department is in charge of salmon while they're in freshwater, but the Commerce Department handles them when they're in saltwater. I hear it gets even more complicated when they're smoked.

In the early years of America's existence, bureaucracy was a good thing. According to *Macrowikinomics* author Don Tapscott, a recognized expert on innovation and technology who's written nine books on the topic, "Bureaucracy was a hot term 90 years ago. It helped us to prevent graft, patronage and corruption. . . . I'm in the center, I push whatever it is out to you, and you're a passive recipient, isolated from others. It's a one-way model. In education, it's *I'm a professor, you're a student*. An empty vessel. In politics, it's *You vote, I rule*."

In the pre-Internet world, this vertically integrated, top-down model worked great, but the Internet revolution turned everything upside down. Ordinary people no longer need the political, social, or media elite to tell them what's happening, what to do, how to vote, how to live. Now they can research, publish, organize, even foment revolution—all without getting up from their laptops or iPads or putting down their smartphones (wireless phones with Web access). The way people approach authority has completely changed, yet the structure of our institutions has stayed exactly the same.

All of this only increases the gap between people and government—a gap that can seem so wide, it's as if government bureaucrats are functioning in a completely different world. When I sat down to talk with venture capitalist Roger Ehrenberg, who spends his time working with entrepreneurs and technologists, he spoke about those in government as if they were a different species. He told me, "I perceive politicians as operating in some parallel universe. I don't know who they are. . . . They're just not understandable. They don't speak like anybody I know." Listening to speeches by any number of politicians, you might find yourself feeling the same way.

So how do we bridge this gap? By embracing the very thing that created it. Technology has rendered our current system of government irrelevant, so now government must turn to technology to fix itself.

I talked with former president Bill Clinton about this when he was in Silicon Valley to address a technology convention, and it turns out he's done a lot of thinking about how technology can transform our bureaucracy. "The great thing about social media is its institutionalized impatience," he told me. "Because the bad thing about bureaucracies is, they can always find a reason not to do something." Yet he said, "For social media to work in governance, it has to be open; it has to be transparent, and people who are in public office have to be really content with wide variations in how many people actually absorb the various things you're putting out." That kind of openness and transparency has never been easy for government, but it's the key to finally entering what Don Tapscott has dubbed the second era of democracy:

> We have an opportunity to move toward a model where citizens get engaged. The first era of democracy was great—it set up these representative institutions. But there was a weak public mandate and an inert citizenry. We can move toward a second era now where you have a culture of public deliberation and active citizenship. If we do that, maybe we can start to break down some of these silos and walls of division that exist now.

New technology has made people more socially active than ever, because they now have the tools to create, communicate, and share in ways they never had before. If we could harness one tenth of the energy that people have spent trying to create the next great smartphone app and direct it toward building tools to improve government, can you imagine the progress we'd make?

You might argue that people build apps because they want to make money selling them. But the reality is, people will build cool things for the sake of building cool things. They will expend countless hours and untold energy for the sake of creating something useful or even just fun. There's an excitement out there, a hunger to try new things, to explore the limits of what all these new technologies can do.

People under the age of thirty grew up with computers, video games, mobile phones—these things are as natural and familiar to the millennial generation as radio, television, and telephones were to earlier generations. The energy to explore is there. So the question is how do we direct some of that energy toward civic life? How do we get people as excited about engaging with government as they are about Angry Birds?

There's tremendous idealism among young people today—they're volunteering, they're engaged, they network. Their compassion is obvious at the local level—they're in their churches, contributing to food banks and volunteering at homeless shelters in record numbers. But their notion of public spirit is completely divorced from politics and government. There's no more "thousand points of light," no real sense of connection between people and government.

Why? Because the level of trust Americans have in politicians and government is so low.

## NATIONAL GOVERNMENT COMING-OUT DAY

Throughout America today, there's a sense of learned helplessness. People don't believe their votes matter. They don't feel that politicians listen to them. They think that no matter what they say or do, everything will stay the same as it has always been.

In the midst of the worst economic crisis in decades, people saw their political leaders not leading but squabbling and name-calling. The rhetoric remains white-hot, and communication between the parties, essential to a functioning democracy, has all but ceased. These days, having a frank, honest discussion with someone from the other side of the aisle is seen as a traitorous act. And people are responding in kind: In December 2011, Gallup found that only 11 percent of Americans approved of the job Congress was doing—the lowest mark ever recorded.

In a *Meet the Press* appearance on September 4, 2011, Thomas Friedman compared America to a space shuttle with two squabbling pilots—Democrats and Republicans—in the cockpit. He contrasted that dysfunction with the great creativity bubbling up from ordinary people:

> I'll tell you what makes me optimistic, is that this country is still full of people who just didn't get the word. And they are starting things and inventing things and creating things and organizing things. If you want to be an optimist about America, stand on your head. You look at this country from the bottom up. You see the potential. We're like the space shuttle, all that thrust coming from below. But right now the booster rocket, Washington, D.C., is cracked and leaking energy. And the pilots in the cockpit are fighting over the flight plan. So we can't achieve the escape velocity we need now to get to the next level. You fix those two things, we take off.

This partisanship and the mistrust of government it breeds are crippling the country. We go through cycles—big government, smaller government, the Occupy movement, the Tea Party—as though we're on a roller coaster. Everyone's dissatisfied, the change that everyone promises is not materializing, and the government is consistently playing in the margins, trying to fail more efficiently. When ordinary people feel politics is irrelevant, the whole Jeffersonian model of democracy is in peril; we're becoming a government of the elites, the opposite of what our forefathers intended, and the opposite of what has historically made America strong.

When people see politicians attacking each other rather than working together, why wouldn't they turn their backs? When "government" is represented by fights over the debt ceiling, shrill arguments over judicial appointments, threats of government shutdowns and sequestration, who would ever want to be part of that? By now, the notion of government is so incredibly distorted that the only way to restore people's trust in it is to go all the way back to basics. We have to make sure people understand that government actually does far more than squabble, posture, obfuscate, and beg for money.

A couple of years ago, an anonymously penned Facebook meme appeared that was written from the point of view of a regular Joe Blow starting his day:

This morning I was awoken by my alarm clock, powered by electricity generated by the public power monopoly regulated by the US Department of Energy. I then took a shower in the clean water provided by the municipal water utility.

After that, I turned on the TV to one of the FCC-regulated channels to see what the National Weather Service of the National Oceanographic and Atmospheric Administration determined the weather was going to be like, using satellites designed, built, and launched by the National Aeronautics and Space Administration.

I watched this while eating a breakfast of US Department of Agriculture–inspected food, and taking drugs which have been determined as safe by the Food and Drug Administration at the appropriate time, as regulated by the US Congress and kept accurate by the National Institute of Standards and Technology and the US Naval Observatory.

I get into my National Highway Traffic Safety Administration–approved automobile and set out to work on the roads built by the local, state, and federal departments of transportation, possibly stopping to purchase additional fuel of a quality level determined by the Environmental Protection Agency, using legal tender issued by the Federal Reserve bank.

On the way out the door I deposit any mail I have to send via the US Postal Service and drop the kids off at the public school. After work, I drive my NHTSA car back home on the DOT roads, to a house which has not burned down in my absence because of the state and local building codes and fire marshal's inspection, and which has not been plundered of all its valuables, thanks to the local police department.

I then log on to the internet, which was developed by the Defense Advanced Research Projects Administration and post on freerepublic .com and Fox News forums about how SOCIALISM in medicine is BAD because the government can't do anything right.

The purpose of this essay, of course, was to counter Republican arguments that President Obama was some kind of radical socialist. But to my mind, it does something even more important. It shows people how much more there is to government than just middle-aged guys spouting partisan poison on Sunday morning talk shows.

Government connects to every part of us—from the air we breathe, to the water we drink, to the lights that are on, to the roads we drive on. We experience government every single day, directly and indirectly. But because government can't brand all its projects with its own little Nike swoosh, people don't realize that fact. Because government doesn't have an official PR department to help burnish its image, people go about their daily lives oblivious to how enriched they are by it.

Clay Shirky, a New York University professor and prominent writer on the Internet and society, calls this the submerged-state argument. "It's one of the reasons we now have people standing up and saying, 'Keep the government's hands off my Medicare!'" he says—no one realizes Medicare's actually a federal program. "The government has gotten incredibly good at service delivery that doesn't look like a government service," he told me. It has managed to create a situation in which it seems to be less important than it is.

Talking to Shirky about the submerged state gave me an idea. Ever since I opened San Francisco's city hall to performing same-sex marriages in 2004, I've been known as a friend of the gay community. One of the community's traditions I most admire is National Coming-Out Day, a day in October when gay men and lesbians are encouraged to tell their friends, families, and coworkers about their sexual orientation.

Well, I'd like to see a national coming-out day for government workers. Almost 23 million Americans work for local, state, or federal government. As the *Wall Street Journal* noted in 2011, that's more people "than work in construction, farming, fishing, forestry, manufacturing, mining, and utilities combined." With approximately 140 million Americans working, government employees represent about 16 percent of the total workforce. Look around you: that's one out of every six people you see.

If all those people stood up one day and said, "We are the government," the rest of the country would be stunned. They'd see that when we talk about government, we're talking about neighbors, family members, acquaintances, friends. Government is not some amorphous, evil "them." Government is *us*. It's the police officer, soldier, educator, IT worker, secretary, lawyer, or engineer who lives next door. Helping people realize that would be a great first step in cutting through the disdain and mistrust people have for government today.

I talked about this idea with Stewart Brand, the legendary founder of the *Whole Earth Catalog* and the man credited with coining the term "personal computer." Brand is one of America's most colorful thinkers, and as we sat in his book-lined office a stone's throw from the water in Sausalito, he said, "We honor soldiers for their service. But we don't honor National Park rangers for their service. And they're close, because they wear military uniforms left over from 1895, I think, is when the military ran the parks. . . ." We need to show respect for the people doing these jobs.

He thought for another moment, then cut to the chase, a smile on his face. "After 9/11, every fireman in the world could get laid for a couple of months. And did. The question is, how do we do that for the guys in the IRS?"

Overcoming bureaucracy, updating the museum pieces of governance, revealing the real people who make up our government, restoring trust: technology can help us do all of these crucial things, if we allow ourselves to embrace it.

# TWO

# Tear Down That Wall!

ONE THING YOU NEVER GET USED to as a politician is seeing yourself burned in effigy. It's happened to me more than once, but the first time was in 2002 when I fought for a new program called Care Not Cash.

At the time, San Francisco had record numbers of homeless, and the amount of our cash assistance to them had gone through the roof. Each person was entitled to almost $400 a month—all you had to do was self-declare as homeless, then go pick up your money on the first and fifteenth of each month at any of dozens of check-cashing facilities in the city.

Our cash assistance was higher than that of any other county or city in California. No one even came close. San Mateo, just south of San Francisco, gave out about $60 a month per person. So not surprisingly, we had a massive migration of homeless into San Francisco—thousands of people who lived in San Mateo County would just walk across the county line to get that extra $340 or so a month. One woman who lived in Reno, Nevada, reportedly took a bus into town every two weeks just to pick up her cash.

This migration created a huge social problem. Invariably, on the first and fifteenth of each month, when the checks were handed out, our emergency rooms, sadly, would be packed with inebriated people.

Ambulances with other sick and injured people had to be diverted because hospitals had no free beds. Crime went up. The costs, both direct and indirect, were enormous—it was a debacle for the city.

San Francisco's homeless advocates resisted any efforts to change the program, and at first I did too. I thought it made sense to provide people the cash they needed to live, and as a county supervisor I even supported increases in the amount of cash aid. But eventually, I couldn't square my own liberal beliefs about helping those in need with my pragmatic desire to actually make things better.

The reality on the streets was that the $400 a month we handed out wasn't improving people's lives. What we needed was a plan to provide people with the care they needed, not just cash. No issue drove my passion more than homelessness, and, in many ways, it defined my two terms as mayor. It was the most obvious and visible expression of our city's inability to solve problems, and I desperately wanted to do something about it.

So I proposed a program—Care Not Cash—that would cut the cash stipend to $59 a month and put the rest directly toward guaranteed housing and services for the homeless. People were outraged. Progressives and Democrats, nuns and priests, homeless advocates and homeless people were furious. But I truly believed, based on the evidence we had, that this was the better way to take care of the city's homeless. It was pragmatism over pure ideology.

We fought for two years to implement Care Not Cash, through ballot initiatives and court battles. And when we finally were able to launch the program, what amazed me was how little hard information we actually had. We'd never done any real data collection on the homelessness problem, and because we had no data, homeless advocates and others could simply claim that things worked poorly or well based on anecdotes. They'd tell stories gleaned from the streets, tapping people's emotions, and then demand that we make public policy based on those anecdotes.

This made no sense. We had no coordinated records system for people checking into shelters. There were no mechanisms in place for tracking people's needs and fulfilling them efficiently. No one in government had any kind of usable, standardized data, so no one could connect the dots—people struggled with mental health issues, substance abuse issues, physical issues, but our efforts to help were scattered and slipshod. How could we solve the problems when we didn't even have any concrete data on what they were?

## PROJECT HOMELESS CONNECT

That was the moment I truly understood the power of data. It may be a dry, boring-sounding word, but real data are fascinating and powerful—a living, breathing, ever-changing picture of people and their needs. In order to truly help the homeless, we first had to understand exactly what their needs were and why those needs weren't being met. And there was no way we could do that when the people responsible for San Francisco's homeless services were stuck behind desks, talking abstractly about what the problems were. We needed to get them out of their offices and into the streets.

So one Friday night, I rounded up a group of city employees, department heads, and a few volunteers, and we headed to one of the city's most underserved communities, the Tenderloin district. We started asking people questions—just talking to them—to find out what their concerns and problems were. We set up tables in a nearby gym and invited people to come in and unload all their concerns. By the end of the evening, everybody was jazzed. This was what real public service was about—getting out of our offices and reaching people on the streets! One deputy department head even said to me, "Thank you for reminding me why I took this job in the first place."

People wanted to do it again, and so we did. We went out for several weeks in a row, and each week, the project—now called Project Homeless Connect—got bigger. We had a dozen volunteers, then a hundred, then three hundred, then a thousand. We moved from that small gym to a gigantic auditorium and got businesses and nonprofits to set up tables and offer free services—everything from legal advice to foot care, eye exams, dental checkups, and acupuncture. Homeless people could come in and get most of their needs taken care of in one place. Everything was under one roof. All the dots were finally connected. And at the same time we were helping people, we were collecting a treasure trove of data. It was the perfect loop.

And yet something was still missing. Once we started collecting all that data, it became obvious that simply collecting it wasn't enough. We needed that information to be accessible, searchable, standardized. Otherwise, it was just a pile of numbers and letters, little more than wasted potential.

That's when the chairman and CEO of the cloud-computing company Salesforce, Marc Benioff, stepped in. "What data system are you using for intake?" he asked me. When I answered that we didn't really have one, he offered to have his company's foundation set up a cloud-computing system for our homelessness efforts. The cloud system would allow us to organize and access data from anywhere, rather than having it stored away in filing cabinets or hard drives.

With Benioff's help, we developed Project Homeless Connect into a thriving homeless-assistance program. Switching to cloud computing enabled us to identify and fulfill people's real needs. We created an endless feedback loop, one that has drastically improved the lives of homeless people in our city.

In the years since we launched Project Homeless Connect, San Francisco's homeless population has declined, emergency room visits have fallen, and deaths from overdoses have plummeted. The project was so successful, it's been replicated in at least 260 cities. And Care Not Cash, so bitterly opposed by homeless advocates, helped result in a 28 percent decline in the homeless population in its very first year. Now, nearly a decade later, the number of homeless people receiving assistance is down more than 80 percent from the pre–Care Not Cash days. And our efforts were significantly advanced by that one word: *data*. A word that, appropriately, is the plural of the Latin *datum*, meaning "given."

## THE CLOUDS ARE GATHERING

We're still in the early days of cloud technology, but soon it will be as ubiquitous as electricity and water. I spoke with Vivek Kundra, President Obama's first chief information officer, in Washington, D.C., and he put it this way: "When you look at how homes were built in the early days, you had your own well for water, and your own generator for electricity. But then we built this massive infrastructure that allowed us to consume and pay per use."

The same thing will happen with the cloud. "On the technology front," Kundra says, "we'll see clouds in the context of how we deliver vital services like health care and education." Just as it did with Homeless Connect, the cloud will enable us to organize and access our data and maximize its effectiveness.

Here's an example of what I mean: In the Bayview neighborhood, one of the poorest in San Francisco, ambulance response time is far slower than in richer neighborhoods. How do we know? Because an enterprising reporter filed a Freedom of Information Act request to get the 911 data. Prior to that information becoming public, residents of Bayview could only complain about isolated incidents and hope someone in government might respond. But once a reporter dug up cold, hard data to confirm their claims, the government had no choice but to act.

Why should this type of data—paid for by our tax dollars—be kept secret from us? The very existence of the Freedom of Information Act, which requires written requests for data that should be openly available, shows how unfree our information really is. The FOIA is a vending-machine approach to government; in the age of the cloud, this kind of data will be available to anyone who cares to search for it online.

New York City put this idea into action in August 2011, when Hurricane Irene slammed into the East Coast. The city's new chief digital officer, Rachel Sterne, loaded up the NYC.gov Web site with maps, evacuation info, real-time photos, and reports, and Mayor Michael Bloomberg encouraged New Yorkers to check in frequently for updates. So many people wanted this information that the NYC.gov Web site crashed for several hours just as the storm swept in.

So what did the city do? Sterne made sure the maps and data were made available to other Web sites, including WNYC.org and NYT .com. "We put it into the public domain," she told me, "so people could use it." When the storm hit, New Yorkers were ready—because they had the data they needed. If New York had kept the data behind the glass of the vending machine, as had happened in years past, it would have helped no one.

There are countless other ways that governments can benefit from releasing data. If a city releases information about bicycle accidents, dangerous intersections can be identified and made safer. If a city releases information about street crime, people can create mash-ups to pinpoint problem areas and times, and police patrols can be increased. If a city releases information about air and water quality or hospital safety or emergency services efficiency, people can make informed decisions that potentially save lives. As Don Tapscott says, "There are thousands of cases where this is happening around the world—but it's not systematic yet." It needs to be.

Making data openly available can even help to avert terrible catastrophes. The entrepreneur and tech blogger Peter Hirshberg suggested that the September 11 attacks might not have happened in an open-data environment. The specific problem, he wrote me in an e-mail, was "the way information flowed in the run-up to 9/11":

> FBI agents in Florida saw that suspicious people were learning to fly jetliners but didn't seem to care about landing them. They emailed this up the chain of command . . . and in South Florida, that chain of command cared a lot about drug interdictions, so the insight didn't go anywhere.
>
> Meanwhile, in San Diego, other agents found suspicious people also engaged in learning out-of-sequence airplane skills. But there was no way for those two groups to connect and, in social media parlance, form a group about "watching people learning to fly airplanes in a very strange manner." Communication lines were linear, rigid, not self-forming.

The results were, of course, catastrophic. So in 2008, the federal government launched a networking site called A-Space—"Facebook for spooks." It's a highly restricted social-media site where the FBI, CIA, NSA, and other intelligence services can share information—a modern networking tool for a networked world. The government also launched Intellipedia—a Wikipedia-style site for spies that Hirshberg describes as "a mechanism where reports from around the world can be aggregated to build encyclopedic knowledge on a subject." Both of these sites are crucial to the business of spycraft in the twenty-first century.

The costs of keeping data hidden are high, sometimes tragically so. But let's look at the flip side—instead of trying to avert catastrophe, what net positive things can we gain from opening up our data? What kind of benefits can greater openness bring us?

## LET THE SUNLIGHT IN

I asked former president Clinton what he thought about open data. The answer he gave had nothing to do with statistics or public policy. It was about trust.

"I basically believe that in a time when people are frustrated, and angry, and mad, and a lot of them have legitimately gotten the shaft, that if you look like you're sharing information and you trust people to draw rational conclusions, your chances of getting to a good outcome are lots better," he said. Then he added that while most people might not care about raw data—"it might make some people cross-eyed bored," he observed—those who do can interpret it and make it useful for the rest of us.

Right now, our government has a credibility problem. It's not trustworthy. Politicians don't always do what they say, and they tend to fall back on scare tactics, political positioning, and posturing. People are sick of the hypocrisy and sick of wondering who's telling the truth and who's telling tales to get themselves reelected.

People would riot if they knew about the private conversations between some politicians. "The public is incapable of understanding the nuances of this, so let's not tell them the whole truth" is an attitude I've heard expressed over and over. Well, that may have worked in the analog world, when we were faxing things and dialing numbers on our rotary phones, but it won't work in this new world, where information has a way of getting out. And that's a good thing.

The Sunlight Foundation was created in 2006 to make government more transparent and accountable. Founders Michael Klein and Ellen Miller were alarmed by the scale of corruption in Washington—from Jack Abramoff's dirty lobbying deals to Tom DeLay's ethical lapses, the business of governing seemed more than ever to be a shady, back-room affair. Yet at the same time, the nascent boom in social net-working meant that Americans were starting to share more and more information than ever. Klein and Miller launched Sunlight to meld these two trends into a movement, shining a light on dark dealings in Washington.

"Confidence in government can't get lower," Ellen Miller told me when I met with her and her Sunlight colleagues at their offices in Wash-ington, D.C. "I do think—and Sunlight operates on this principle—that transparency will increase trust. . . . I don't think it will be an immediate process. But people get angry, and then they take further action. It all starts with information." The more we know about what our politicians are doing, the more inclined they'll be to behave honorably—because it's just human nature to behave better when someone is watching.

Transparency is also the best way to combat one of the biggest problems our country faces today: the special-interest money that's corrupting politics all across America. "If you generally ask the American people, 'What's wrong with politics today?' they'll say, 'There's too much money,'" Miller told me. "The notion that Wall Street, because it gives so much money, has too much power just fits into something they've been feeling for years. But how do you get to a solution?"

Sunlight's answer: data. "Most of our work focuses on money-power-politics," says Miller. "We build tools and Web sites to connect the data." She cites the example of the Web site influenceexplorer.com, which details campaign contributions at the federal and state levels. With these types of tools offering easy, searchable ways to find data on campaign finance, lobbying, earmarks, and the like, people can see for themselves who's been dealing with whom. The data makes candidates and elected officials accountable—even if they don't want to be.

One congressional staffer remarked on the vast difference between those who are required to publicly report spending and those who aren't. "In terms of spending," he told me, "Congress is the most transparent institution in the federal government. If we buy a piece of candy, it's reported and online. That's the way we live. But when I look at the executive branch, the Department of Energy, the Department of Defense, they line-item by the millions." And who knows what those millions are really going for?

That discrepancy was never more vividly illustrated than in the General Services Administration scandal of 2012, when it was discovered that GSA staffers had spent more than $800,000 on a junket to Las Vegas—complete with a mind reader, clowns, and a red-carpet party. We can only assume that, had they known in advance that the details of their spending would be made public, they most likely would have chosen to spend more wisely. The simple truth is, if you know you must reveal your spending publicly, you're more likely to think twice about how you spend. Transparency leads to trust.

## THE AGE OF BIG DATA

In 2001, a small group of entrepreneurs founded a company called Keyhole. It started developing several different products, but the one that seemed most promising was something called Earth Viewer. The idea was simple but intriguing: using Earth Viewer, people could zoom in on satellite imagery of the entire earth, including close-ups, all while sitting right at their computers. In fact, the founders chose the name Keyhole in honor of the KH reconnaissance satellite system, a CIA system used to spy on the Soviet Union during the cold war.

The developers at Keyhole worked on Earth Viewer for three years. Then, in 2004, Google bought the young company, renaming its product Google Earth. The price of the acquisition has never been reported, but it's safe to assume that the founders made many millions of dollars.

Why is this important? Because it perfectly illustrates another potentially enormous benefit of opening up government data. Keyhole used government data—the images captured by government satellites—to create a hugely successful commercial product. Millions of dollars were generated, jobs were created, and consumers got a tremendously useful product. It was a win-win-win situation.

Satellite data has been used to build numerous global positioning system (GPS) products, and it has also spawned another useful and profitable industry: weather forecasting. The decision during the Reagan administration to open up satellite data led to the success of Accu-Weather and many other, smaller companies. Information that was once held tightly by the National Oceanic and Atmospheric Agency (NOAA) was made available for public use, and the effect was immediate. Once again, thousands of jobs were created, money was made, and consumers benefited.

We paid for that data with our tax dollars. It belongs to the public, and we should be able to access and use it. Some might argue that allowing people to make money from government data is wrong or inappropriate. But can anyone really argue that we're worse off, in any way, for having easy access to accurate weather information and commercial GPS? The switch to consumer weather forecasting was so seamless and so successful that one clueless congressman actually suggested abolishing NOAA, asking, "Why do we need it when we have the Weather Channel?"

Microsoft's director of innovative engagement, Mark Drapeau, wonders why more entrepreneurs don't take advantage of government data for new businesses. In a *Fast Company* article called "Government Social Media: Five Questions for 2011," he asked, "Where are the open government entrepreneurs?"

> If you're an entrepreneur, isn't a long-lasting, successful, well-known company and trusted brand precisely what you strive for as a goal? And yet, it's rare to hear a discussion among entrepreneurs who have that kind of vision in the government space. Everyone seems to be a consultant of some kind. There's nothing wrong with consulting the government on open data, or social media, or whatever. But where are the MBA's and VC's?

When I spoke with Drapeau about this problem, he said, "There's a lot of data out there, but very few actual entrepreneurs trying to make money off it. And the ones that are are pretty low profile. I don't entirely get it." Something's not adding up: "We have all this unemployment, underemployed people, and so on, and it's never been easier to find data, use it, talk about it—and there's seemingly no intersection between these two big things." Perhaps entrepreneurs just don't think about government data as a commercial resource. In a twenty-first-century government model, that too must change.

Vivek Kundra is a huge proponent of this idea. "Look at NIH, for example," he told me, referring to the National Institutes of Health. "The NIH and other world bodies worked on decoding the human genome. Scientists from around the world who were working on the genome project convened in Bermuda and issued what became known as the Bermuda accords. They made all the data open and public," Kundra said. "Scientists would share and give back to the pool. That's what government should be about now—creating the common wealth."

As a result of the Bermuda accords, there has been an "explosion in personalized medicine," Kundra noted. "It's the best of how government and the private sector should work. Create an investment in R & D, then the private sector creates a business. . . . VC's put money into genomics because they can sell it. How do we do this with government products?"

Kundra suggests a VC incubator that makes big bets on government data—a venture fund to bankroll highly regulated markets. "It's a win-win message for the Democrats," he said. "Private markets come in, and you create this perfect ecosystem of third parties creating value based on government data that the American people have already paid for."

Making such incubators work is easier said than done, of course.

And while there's a lot of excitement around the idea of government-affiliated incubators these days, there's also a growing sense that this may be a bubble about to pop. The factors that contribute to VC success—time-intensive mentoring, networking, and risk taking—aren't hallmarks of government, so we must tread carefully in this sphere. The notion of one "home run" paying for many failures works only if that home run actually happens, so we must delve into this field only if we can provide the proper tools for success.

On the other hand, instead of injecting VC practices into government, why not inject government into the VC world? Open up the competition for government services and encourage the development of start-ups that address the big, thorny, hard-to-solve issues that plague government today. Let's remove any obstacles that keep traditional incubators—private VC firms—from creating these new companies and help them get a foothold in solving government service problems.

Creating new companies isn't the only way government data can help boost the economy. As Bill Clinton told me, "I predict this [open data] will create a whole new class of employment demand, which is data sifters." There's such a wealth of data out there that we're going to need people who can sort the wheat from the chaff. Clinton foresees a need even for something as basic as sifting through the thousands of e-mails constituents send to their elected officials.

"You owe it to the public" to effectively sort through constituents' ideas, he told me. "How do you train people so they'll know the difference between something that sounds good but won't work and something that sounds good and will make a huge change?" This is a big responsibility, but it's an opportunity too.

In a February 2012 story, the *New York Times* dubbed this the age of big data and described the employment boom that could result:

A report last year by the McKinsey Global Institute, the research arm of the consulting firm [McKinsey], projected that the United States needs 140,000 to 190,000 more workers with "deep analytical" expertise and 1.5 million more data-literate managers, whether retrained or hired. . . . There is a lot more data, all the time, growing at 50 percent a year, or more than doubling every two years, estimates IDC, a technology research firm. . . .

"It's a revolution," says Gary King, director of Harvard's Institute for Quantitative Social Science. "We're really just getting under way. But the march of quantification, made possible by enormous new sources of data, will sweep through academia, business and government. There is no area that is going to be untouched."

This move toward open data and cloud technology is launching a whole new industry. "It's going to be very painful," Roger Ehrenberg told me, "but it's also going to be a huge job-creation opportunity."

## IT USED TO BE "BIG BROTHER IS WATCHING YOU"

So far, we've seen that opening up our data will (1) create more trust in government, (2) provide opportunities for entrepreneurs, and (3) create jobs. There's a fourth benefit: Open data empowers people.

Wim Elfrink of Cisco Systems notes, "In the past, if you were the one sitting on data, you were in control." The boss always had more information than the employee. The elected official always had more information than the voter. The police had more information than the citizens. The dictator had more information than the people he ruled.

"It used to be 'Big Brother is watching you,'" Elfrink went on.

"Now, it's 'We, the citizens, are watching *you*.'" We've seen this time and again in the age of cell-phone cameras and YouTube: A candidate is caught making a racial slur, or police officers are videoed pepper-spraying a group of peacefully seated student protestors. The easier it is for ordinary people to collect information, the greater their power.

"We are seeing actually what I think of as a new ideology," says the futurist Peter Schwartz. "It's the ideology of social organization from the bottom, and the right to take power because you can do things you couldn't do before. It legitimates the capacity to organize." This capacity is enabled by information, by the network. Schwartz pointed to the summer 2011 protests in San Francisco as an example of citizen empowerment—and the government's attempts to quash it.

On July 3 of that summer, a Bay Area Rapid Transit (BART) police officer fatally shot a homeless man named Charles Hill after he had allegedly brandished two knives. Witnesses claimed Hill had posed no threat, and the story blew up on blogs, Twitter, and Facebook.

A video of the shooting released in late July further convinced people that Hill hadn't posed a lethal threat, and anger at the BART police flared higher. On August 11, a group named Anonymous called for protestors to shut down four BART stations in downtown San Francisco. Armed with information on the shooting and with the help of cell phones and social networking, people were taking power into their own hands.

But on August 11, the BART staff shut down power to the cell phone nodes in the four stations, taking away the protestors' ability to communicate with each other. The planned shutdowns never took place, which the BART staff might have considered a victory, at least at first. Yet while they won that battle, they lost the ensuing war. The shutdown was seen as a heavy-handed, dictatorial crackdown, and it ignited a firestorm.

In an article titled "BART Pulls a Mubarak in San Francisco," the Electronic Frontier Foundation had this to say:

> This week, EFF has seen censorship stories move closer and closer to home—first Iran, then the UK, and now San Francisco, an early locus of the modern free speech movement. . . . Cutting off cell phone service in response to a planned protest is a shameful attack on free speech. BART officials are showing themselves to be of a mind with the former president of Egypt, Hosni Mubarak, who ordered the shutdown of cell phone service in Tahrir Square in response to peaceful, democratic protests earlier this year.

The outcry against BART's actions was loud and sustained, and the system's leadership responded. "It's no longer a BART issue, it's a nationwide issue and the public has to weigh in on it," said BART board member Bob Franklin. "That's the difference between our country and other countries. We will have a public dialogue on this and talk about an appropriate use, if it is appropriate."

Four days later, Anonymous rescheduled the shutdown. BART staff left the cell-phone nodes on, and the shutdown of four stations turned San Francisco's evening commute into a snarled, frustrating mess. The people had taken power into their own hands—with data and networks aiding them every step of the way.

"Before, political organization had to be relatively hierarchical," says Schwartz. "It was all about communication and control. What this new medium has done is to take power from the center and distribute it rather radically." Those in authority may not like it, but this is the wave of the future, and they're going to have to deal with it. "This is a multidecade transformation, generational in character," says Schwartz. "That is the emerging reality of governance."

# THE FILTER BUBBLE

In 1992, several years before I went into politics, I opened a wine store called PlumpJack in San Francisco—the first in a series of PlumpJack properties that would come to include restaurants, hotels, and wineries. Soon after opening that first store, we began posting reviews for our customers. In the wine business, there are two reviewers whose scores matter: Robert Parker and the *Wine Spectator*. They grade wines and vintages on a hundred-point scale, and stores will usually post the higher of the two scores to convince customers a wine is good in hopes that they'll buy more of it.

But I didn't like the idea of giving customers only one-sided information. In fact, I decided that the only scores we would post were for vintages about which the reviewers completely disagreed. We only posted scores in PlumpJack that were at least ten points apart for the same wine. Robert Parker loves this wine, but *Wine Spectator* hates it: What do *you* think? After all, there's really no such thing as an objectively good or bad wine—in the end, it's all subjective. We wanted people to make up their own minds and not be influenced by the so-called experts. By giving them information in an unfiltered way, we wanted to empower them.

Now imagine that Robert Parker and the *Wine Spectator* are the editorial boards of the *New York Times* and the *Wall Street Journal,* or MSNBC and Fox News, or ThinkProgress.org and RedState.com. On any given day, if you get your opinions from one source and not the other, you're getting only half the story. You'll be getting fed one point of view, not developing your own based on competing information. And you'll be missing out on the whole spectrum of what's out there.

Many people choose to rely on just one side for their information.

That's their prerogative. But even those who *do* want to hear all sides are now being denied the opportunity—by Google, Facebook, and other search and social-media sites. And we don't even realize it. The dirty little secret is that each of us is perched in the middle of something called the Filter Bubble.

Eli Pariser, the board president of MoveOn.org and author of *The Filter Bubble*, gave a Technology, Entertainment, Design (TED) conference talk in which he explained how the most prominent Internet companies deny us certain kinds of information. He described noticing one day that, even though he has Facebook friends of all political persuasions, his Facebook News Feed had eliminated updates from his conservative friends. "Facebook was looking at which links I clicked on," he said, "and it was noticing that I was clicking more on my liberal friends' links than my conservative friends' links. And without consulting me about it, it had edited them out."

Google, he explained, did something similar. "If I search for something and you search for something, even right now at the very same time, we might get very different search results." According to Pariser, Google assesses fifty-seven different "signals"—from what computer and browser you're using to where you're physically located—to help determine which search results you see. Though most people don't know it, there's no such thing as a standard Google search result. Everything is personalized.

The problem with this, as Pariser notes, is that it "moves us quickly toward a world in which the Internet shows us what we *want* to see, but not necessarily what we *need* to see." And the decisions are being made not by human editors with ethical codes, but by computer algorithms that merely crunch numbers. The highest good for these algorithms is "relevance." But in an ethically complex world, relevance shouldn't be the only factor deciding what you're exposed to. As Pariser says, you can't have a functioning democracy if citizens don't have a flow of information.

We no longer live in a world where Walter Cronkite is the single voice of news for all Americans. We no longer live in a world where everyone in a city reads the local newspaper and the front-page story is the same for everyone. Today people get their news, information, and opinions from thousands of different sources—Web sites, blogs, cable channels, Twitter feeds. . . . That's not going to change, nor should it. But we have to strive toward making sure that raw information is available to everyone, so people can make their own decisions. This, too, is the promise of open data.

## THE PEOPLE'S DATA

The final argument for opening up data isn't about whatever good things we can gain from it. It's about the fact that opening up government data is just the right thing to do. We paid for it. We own it. We have a right to it.

A couple of summers ago, as a member of the Board of Regents, I was at a meeting for the University of California system when a spirited debate broke out about how to avoid tuition increases. The state's budget had been slashed, and the financial outlook was grim. How could we bring enough money into the system so that students and their families didn't get squeezed?

One of the regents suggested that we ramp up the licensing of research being done at UC research labs to our commercial contracts with the private sector, so we agreed to convene a work group on commercializing university research. Yet while I do believe we should make data available, there's a gray area with this kind of research. I suggested to my fellow regents that this wasn't really our data to sell: "It's research done by public employees, funded by public dollars," I said. "And now we're going to monetize it like we're a private entity? Who are we to do that?" I was concerned that we weren't respecting the true ownership of the data.

The same thing holds true for all data the government collects, develops, or researches. All persons and agencies funded by taxpayer dollars are *your* employees. They work for you, and the information they produce is owned by you—which means they shouldn't be able to sell it. Just as with the NOAA data, we can open it up and make it available for commercial use, as our default should always be to get the information out there. But open data means just that: *open* data, not data for sale.

As Vivek Kundra says, "We need a policy framework to shift data to the individual. . . . The default should be that you own that information." Kundra gets particularly riled when talking about how hard it is to get his own information. "The IRS—it's crazy that I have to go to my accountant to find out what I filed for the last seven years. Why can't I get the IRS to tell me?"

But governments will always err on the side of releasing the minimum amount of data they can get away with. At a meeting with the State Lands Commission, which I chair as lieutenant governor, we discussed issuing a directive requiring the commission to release years of data—maps and information on parks, roads, and land use. The whole conversation was just pushback from the staff: "Well, how much are you suggesting we release?" And "We've already released $x$, $y$, and $z$," and "We'll get back to you with some ideas."

It's not up to us to "determine what's appropriate." If there's a potential security threat, that's one thing; otherwise, let's put all the data out there. Public hearings, showing our meetings on public-access TV—these aren't enough. We need crunchable, searchable data sets online, not foot dragging and obfuscation. These data sets are not ours to hide. They are the people's to use as they wish.

## TEAR DOWN THAT WALL!

In a 1987 speech at Berlin's Brandenburg Gate, President Ronald Reagan issued a challenge to Soviet leader Mikhail Gorbachev. The Soviet empire had entered a time of turmoil, not only economically, but culturally, too, as Western movies, TV shows, and music were infiltrating the countries behind the Iron Curtain. The Berlin Wall had stood as a barrier between East and West since 1961, and Reagan bluntly urged Gorbachev to do away with it.

"Mr. Gorbachev," he said in the speech's most famous line, "tear down this wall!" I love Reagan's phrase, because it was aimed at knocking down barriers to the free exchange of information, ideas, and culture. And that's what we have to do in this new digital age—we must "tear down that wall" and open up our data for all to share.

But it's not enough simply to pull reams of government data out of filing cabinets. We must do four things with it. We must make sure it is (1) findable, (2) standardized, and (3) trustworthy. Finally, we must (4) make sure there is a narrative to it—a way for people to relate to and use it.

First, data must be **findable**. I was talking with Aneesh Chopra, the first chief technology officer of the Obama administration, who told me about a problem with student-loan data. "We have forever published open data on student loan default rates," he said. "But only researchers know it exists. We haven't told the Silicon Valley crowd"—the people who could create tools for making the data useful. "So the data's not helping students. It's like a chopped tree in the woods—no one knew it existed."

If people can't find data or never know it exists, it's as useless as if it never did exist. Through government Web sites, Facebook pages, Twitter feeds, press releases, memos—whatever it takes—we must make sure that people who can benefit from data sets know that they're out there.

Second, data must be **standardized**. Representative Darrell Issa took a big step toward this goal with his Digital Accountability and Transparency Act of 2011, which would require consistent governmentwide data standards. Why is this so important? Because there are so many different kinds of technologies, computer languages, codes, tags, spreadsheets, and documentation, it's extremely difficult—if not impossible—to find and use data.

If you've ever been unable to open a file someone sent you, or watch a video or see a photo, you know how frustrating different standards can be. If you've ever opened a document or spreadsheet to find mumbo jumbo rather than the cleanly laid-out information you were seeking, you've already seen how important it is to have compatible standards. If we standardize our data now, we can also standardize one conversion technique so we can update and continue to use data into the future, throughout the inevitable introduction of new computer technologies. This is a big undertaking, but it will solve much bigger problems down the road.

Third, we must determine which data are **trustworthy**. Craig Newmark, founder of Craigslist, is particularly focused on this issue. "Trustworthiness is the big idea," he told me. "We need tools that can be used to build identities and positions that are trustworthy." He cites organizations such as GuideStar and GreatNonprofits.org, which rate the trustworthiness of nonprofit organizations, as models. "It's like Yelp for nonprofits," he says. Similarly, we need to ensure that the data sets put out by the government are trustworthy too.

Shawn Allen of the San Francisco Web design company Stamen .com refers to this as "data as conversation. It's not a document that you publish somewhere, but a narrative. It all has a history—who made it, why, and how. We should know the history of those datasets over time." Just as former president Bill Clinton suggested the creation of data sifters as a new class of employment, we should also look to data validaters, who would function in much the same way as Wikipedia's armies of editors.

"There are lots of silly spreadsheets lingering at DataSF.org"— San Francisco's online repository of government data—"because people don't know where they came from or what they're for," says Allen. "There's a latent desire for people to do stuff with data—if they know where it came from."

Finally, open data needs a narrative to be truly useful. "Transparency is not enough," Clay Shirky told me. "Citizens don't consume facts; they consume stories. . . . Access to data is considerably less valuable than access to data *plus* the ability to tell the story of why it matters."

As an example, he cited a scandal in the blue-collar town of Bell, California, where city officials were found to have astronomically higher salaries than their counterparts in other cities. The numbers had been out there, but no one paid any attention until two reporters from the *Los Angeles Times* wrote about it, telling the story behind the data. "The piece I'm interested in," says Shirky, "is not just the availability of the data, but how it translates into civic engagement."

We are, as Vivek Kundra likes to say, in the very early "Friendster version" of open data. Matt Lira agrees. "As a government employee," Lira told me, "I'm surprised by how much progress has been made. But as a technologist, it's not nearly enough." And in today's hyperconnected world, the technologist's standard is the one we must adhere to.

"I think the public is used to this online access to information," says Ellen Miller. "I can buy a book at two A.M. I can order shoes today and have them tomorrow. That same 24/7 access to information is now permeating the political world. . . . Our larger goal is to change the culture of government to do what it doesn't want to do, which is to make information and data about its work and activities publicly accessible."

# THREE

## Living in a Glass House

ON JANUARY 21, 2009, the day after being sworn in, President Obama released a memorandum on transparency and data. To most people's surprise, it advocated throwing wide the curtains of secrecy that often surround government work. "My Administration is committed to creating an unprecedented level of openness in Government," the memo read. "We will work together to ensure the public trust and establish a system of transparency, public participation, and collaboration."

The memo listed three recommendations. First:

Government should be transparent. . . . My administration will take appropriate action, consistent with law and policy, to disclose information rapidly in forms that the public can readily find and use.

Second:

Government should be participatory. . . . Executive departments and agencies should offer Americans increased opportunities to participate in policymaking and to provide their government with the benefits of their collective expertise and information.

And third:

> Government should be collaborative. . . . Executive departments and
> agencies should use innovative tools, methods, and systems to coop-
> erate among themselves, across all levels of government, and with
> nonprofit organizations, businesses and individuals in the private
> sector.

Open-government proponents rejoiced—this memo sounded like
something an advocate would write, not a politician, yet it was coming
straight from the White House! This was like a trumpet blast heralding a new era of openness and accountability in Washington.

Unfortunately, the euphoria didn't last long. The memo was just
that—a memo. It suggested things the administration would like to
see happen, but it offered no teeth to make them happen.

As Ellen Miller of the Sunlight Foundation put it, "The memorandum was fine, but then the White House didn't really follow through.
Our initial relationship with them was 'go go go,' but now it's more
push-pull. Data wasn't forthcoming. The administration said to the
agencies, 'Give us three sets of high-value data.' Well, the agencies put
up data, but whether it was 'high-value' is debatable." For example,
the Department of the Interior, a treasure trove of valuable data on
subjects such as mine safety, climate change, and oil spills, chose to put
up . . . its wild horse and burro count. "High-value" data, indeed.

Some agencies did respond with valuable data, but the memo had
put no real mechanism in place for enforcing data quality or its regular
release, and the Obama administration didn't engage any further.
"[The memo] was nearly perfect as crafted," Miller told me. "It raised
the flag: this is what we're aiming toward. But the progress toward
achieving it has been remarkably slow."

# SINCE WHEN IS TRANSPARENCY
# A RADICAL NOTION?

As mayor and now as lieutenant governor, I've heard every possible reason from agencies as to why they can't release data. "We don't have the money!" Or "We're short staffed!" Or "It's in boxes, and we just moved offices, so we can't get to it!" Or "The person who was doing this retired, and she's the only person who knows where stuff is!" Or "Can't we just wait until audits are done? We don't have time right now for anything else."

Behind the scenes, there's always a mad scramble to figure out the absolute minimum that agencies can get away with releasing or how they might postpone releasing anything until we presumably get distracted and move on to something else. The foot dragging and excuse making are rampant. But why the reluctance? What is everyone afraid of?

In part, it's just a holdover from history. Our government has never been transparent, and there was never, until now, any expectation that it would be. While he was a senator, Barack Obama was among the skeptics, according to Ellen Miller. "When he went to the Senate, he was the point man for post-Abramoff election reforms," she told me. "He held a meeting of reformers. I said to him, 'I think members of Congress should post their official calendars online, so we know whom they're meeting with.'"

Senator Obama's response, according to Miller: "Have you always been a radical?"

"Since when is transparency a radical notion?" Miller wants to know. Apparently, for many in government, it still is.

And yet I can't really blame anyone else for being reluctant to release data, because I've been reluctant to do so myself. While I was mayor, I told my staff I wanted to put my calendar online. Speeches, press conferences, public appearances, private meetings—I wanted everything out there. "Even your fund-raising meetings?" my chief of staff asked, his eyebrows raised. And that stopped me dead.

The truth is, you can't be an elected official in this country if you don't raise money. There are a very few superrich candidates who can afford to fund-raise less than the rest of us, but everyone has to do it. And the process itself is fraught. People don't like the idea of their elected officials spending time soliciting funds, and the whole process, fairly or unfairly, feels unseemly. How would it look if, in a particularly busy fund-raising period, I had multiple private meetings with potential donors? Fund-raising may be a necessary part of politics in this country, but that doesn't make it any more palatable.

And there are other people, not just donors, who also aren't particularly happy about having their private meetings made public. As I immediately realized, it's a lot easier to talk about total openness than to practice it. I wanted to walk the walk, but it would be difficult to do without causing harm to my office or to other people—people such as labor negotiators or business interests, who for their own reasons might not want to broadcast that they were meeting with the mayor.

In theory, I wanted to be totally transparent. But in the end I, too, compromised. Instead of listing meetings by whom we were meeting with, we listed them by topics discussed. In the interest of privacy, we made small changes in the description of meetings. These were cosmetic changes, and even writing about them here is my effort to be more open about them. But the bottom line was, I compromised. So I'm not perfect either.

There are other problems associated with releasing data. In June 2012, the *San Francisco Chronicle* asked to see my schedule for the previous March, April, and May. My office got on it, but unfortunately the request came on my scheduler's final day of working for us. Because I receive so many requests, scheduling is coordinated by one person to keep everything straight, so losing her as the request came in complicated things. We hadn't yet hired a new scheduler, so my overworked staff of three tried to patch together the schedule for those three months. Yet even though they were within the window of reasonable (and legally acceptable) response time, the *Chronicle* pounced, accusing us of withholding information.

With today's technology, sending a schedule should be as easy as pushing a SEND button. Unfortunately, at least in the California lieutenant governor's office, it's not. But the *Chronicle*'s rush to accuse us of wrongdoing is the perfect example of another reason why politicians are reluctant to give up information: It often ends up being used against them. Historically, people who request data or information aren't doing it because they want to solve a problem or create a program. They're often doing it for political purposes, as a kind of "gotcha government."

Here's one example. As mayor, I launched a program called SF Stat, modeled on a program started in Baltimore called CitiStat, which was followed by New York City's CompStat. CompStat was the first government entity to cross data with mapping tools, resulting in a way to map crimes happening in the city. This tool led to all kinds of public good—greater awareness of crime hot spots, increased police presence, and a subsequent reduction in crime.

I wanted to do the same for San Francisco, so we launched SF Stat in 2004, aiming to make public all kinds of data—not just crimes—about the city. Civil service, pensions, budgets, technology—we put everything out on the table for the public to see, in hopes of shining a light on what needed improving.

At those early department-head meetings, not one person understood why I wanted to do this. I said, "This is not a 'gotcha' request. This is a way of empowering you to do your job more effectively." But no one believed me. They were just stewing over the fact that they'd have to release data that would invariably be pored over and criticized by citizens and the media.

Unfortunately, those department heads weren't wrong. We started having SF Stat meetings every other Friday, and they were open to the public. I was excited to open up our data to the people, to show them we were serious about making ourselves accountable and cleaning up government. Following Baltimore's example, we were one of the first cities to open up our data this way, putting it online and holding those Friday meetings to announce what we were up to.

But inevitably, every other Saturday there would be a critical piece in one of our two major daily newspapers about the data we released. If 95 percent of the data showed improvements in the city, the 5 percent that showed something negative was the focus of the article. I'd pick up the paper to read breathless headlines saying something like SAN FRANCISCO DATA SHOWS OVERTIME UP 12 PERCENT—while the fact that the overtime was a necessary response to a spike in crime was buried deep in the article.

Before we opened up our data, reporters wouldn't have found out about the overtime spike until months had passed. But because we took it upon ourselves to make the information readily available, reporters took the opportunity to seek out any whiff of scandal they could. You couldn't blame our department heads for thinking, *Why the heck are we doing this?* This is a major reason behind bureaucratic and political resistance to openness: Why hand someone data that they're just going to use against you?

And believe me, that openness eventually took its toll. The relentless drumbeat of criticism finally wore down my staff and department heads to the point where we were having serious morale problems. It felt as though there was no positive incentive for having those open meetings, and we eventually stopped doing them altogether.

The sad truth is, anytime you put information out there and make it easily accessible, you pay a price. Scandals sell, problems sell, and people don't buy good news. We tried hard to open up our data, but in the end we failed—which is not an acceptable outcome. We must find a way to bring out the positive aspects of data and weather the inevitable criticism, because data's too important to hide.

## YOUTUBE = MEBORED?

It was the same story when I decided to update my State of the City address for the digital age. Normally, a State of the City speech is about an hour long, a general summary of what's been happening over the previous twelve months and a preview of priorities for the new year. But as I prepared for my 2008 speech, I realized that we didn't have to be limited to that time frame. Why not put even more information out there? Why not offer several different in-depth speeches about important topics, such as housing, the environment, and education, rather than covering them in just a few lines in the one main speech?

This seemed like a good idea—who could object to a government official giving out *more* information? And in the age of YouTube, it was incredibly easy to do. I just recorded and posted several different addresses, each focusing on a specific theme. We rolled them out every few days, like webisodes, and responded to comments. Anyone who wanted a deeper look at one of these critical subjects could watch that particular speech online and comment. If you didn't want to, you didn't have to. It's a no-brainer, right?

Wrong. These in-depth State of the City speeches got people riled up beyond reason. In a *San Francisco Examiner* article titled "YouTube = MeBored," columnist Melissa Griffin pilloried me for the videos, quoting a friend who said, "I wouldn't watch Pamela Anderson for 7½ hours, much less Gavin Newsom." More than one writer, including a *New York Times* blogger, compared me to Fidel Castro (for good measure, he also compared me to Mao and Khrushchev).

I got pummeled for the videos, but I'm still proud that they offered people a more comprehensive overview than they'd ever gotten before. I got more hits on those State of the City addresses than some governors get on their State of the States, and for that reason I would do it all over again. But that experience also shows why most politicians are reluctant to put more than the minimum out for the public eye.

In asking public figures to release more information, we're asking them to risk scorn and public ridicule. This is the number-one challenge of the open-data movement, in my opinion—the reason why it hasn't taken off as it should. People are afraid to be skewered. We're asking them to do the one thing that historically has come at a huge cost. It's a monumental mind shift to convince government bureaucrats and politicians of the positive power of this movement. But we must.

And it's not just fear of embarrassment that we have to fight. There's also something Vivek Kundra calls the IT Cartel. "A closed system preserves the status quo," he told me. "In the information economy, information is power"—and those who have power are naturally reluctant to give it up. In an op-ed for the *New York Times*, Kundra wrote about the IT Cartel, government contractors who milk the current system for contracts and fees even as a comprehensive move to cloud computing would make them unnecessary and save taxpayers untold millions of dollars.

"Their whole model is throwing bodies at the problem," Kundra said. "It's 'Land and expand.' They may even *want* to lose money. The government often doesn't have the talent or capacity to manage them—they're just throwing consultant after consultant at the problems.

"Government's problem as a buyer," he went on, "is that it doesn't have the talent to manage contracts. Companies don't feel the Darwinian pressure to innovate. If Google said tomorrow, 'We're not going to optimize search or move into mobile,' they'd be dead. But these guys don't fear that."

Moving from our antiquated government systems to the cloud would solve many of these problems. As Kundra put it in his op-ed, it's the difference between "hardware and software that individuals, businesses and governments buy and then maintain themselves," versus "low-cost, maintenance-free services that are based on the Internet and run by private companies." When the General Services Administration introduced cloud computing, Kundra reveals, the agency cut the costs of its e-mail system by more than half. These are the kinds of success stories we must embrace and emulate.

So in the summer of 2011, I decided to put my money where my mouth was and migrate all the data in the lieutenant governor's office to the cloud—the first statewide office in California to do it. Some of my staff weren't so keen on the idea, but one person was: our twenty-one-year-old intern, John Hewitt.

John was between his sophomore and junior years of college that summer, and he was in the midst of a typical internship—answering phones, filing paperwork, writing certificates of commendation for constituents. Because he was twenty-one, John had literally never known a world without the Internet—he's a digital native. When we talked to him about migrating our data to the cloud, he was eager to help us do it.

For John, it would be a lesson in government bureaucracy he wouldn't forget. "I didn't get any pushback from the lieutenant governor's staff," he said, "but I did get it from the IT department. If you want to download a certain desktop client, you have to call them first. There are a lot of different checks, things you have to go through when it's really quite simple."

John had taken government classes at the University of San Francisco, but seeing how government functions close up was different. "I didn't realize—everyone's so quick to judge, when the legislature has a hard time getting anything done. But when you look at the steps required for something so simple as getting a desktop piece, you realize why everything [in government] takes so long."

Yet the traditional IT department, which set up and maintained complex, centralized services—networks, servers, computers, e-mail, printers—may be on its way out. When the computer revolution began, IT departments were truly needed, as people had no idea how to set up and use the new technologies that were infiltrating their work space. Faced with a jumble of Ethernet cables, modems, printers, and phone lines, the average person would get frustrated trying to make everything work. IT departments were created to help maintain all these tools and technologies.

But these days things are different, as Jason Hiner wrote on Tech Republic.com:

Most of these technologies run themselves today and don't require a lot of time from IT pros to deploy them and keep them running. IT pros also spend a lot less time doing repairs, maintenance, and end user support. Replacement is the new support. In 2015, employees will just swap out their malfunctioning laptop, smartphone, or tablet to IT and immediately get a replacement device that will connect to the private cloud and/or public cloud and instantly download the user's apps, settings, and data.

In the view of Hiner and many others, the traditional IT department is a relic. As we move toward the cloud and technology gets easier to use, we'll have less need for full-time teams of people to maintain our stuff.

There was one other reason the IT staff resisted moving the lieutenant governor's office to the cloud, according to John. "It seems silly to me," he said, "but there's always that one argument that 'For security purposes, we can't do this because something happened one time. . . .' So they have this other layer because 'something happened.' But in reality, that hurts more than it helps."

Yet security is obviously a very real concern—in fact, it's the biggest concern about opening up data and moving to the cloud. But how serious is the problem? As with everything else in this new technological world, it depends on whom you ask—as I found out firsthand after one public disaster.

## PRIVACY VERSUS PUBLIC SAFETY

It was a Thursday evening in the fall of 2010. Two miles from San Francisco International Airport, people in the Crestmoor neighborhood of San Bruno were going about their usual business—making dinner, mowing the lawn, walking their dogs. Suddenly, a violent explosion tore through the quiet, sending a tower of flames hundreds of feet into the air and shaking the ground with the force of a small earthquake.

Panicked residents had no idea what had happened. Did a plane crash? Had someone set off a bomb? The fire ignited nearby homes, and before firefighters could get it under control, thirty-eight homes had been destroyed and more than a hundred others damaged. Eight people died, dozens were injured, and the explosion left a crater more than 160 feet long. The cause: a gas pipe running underneath the neighborhood had blown up. The ensuing fire was fed for hours by gas spewing out of the ruptured pipe.

For residents, this was in some ways more frightening than a plane crash or a bomb—these pipes run through the ground beneath San Bruno, connecting all through San Francisco. After the initial shock wore off, people wanted to know: Is there a gas pipe running underneath my home? Is my neighborhood safe? As it turned out, there were two hundred miles of major pipeline running under San Francisco that needed to be replaced—was it possible that any of those might blow up too?

Pacific Gas and Electric Company (PG&E) didn't want to release information on where exactly those pipes ran, saying that criminals or terrorists might use it to plan an attack. A map on the utility's Web site showed a general schematic for how the pipes ran, but it didn't identify which streets they were under. PG&E's penchant for secrecy was so strong that not even the San Francisco Fire Department knew exactly where the pipes ran. Fire Department spokesperson Lieutenant Mindy Talmadge was quoted saying, "I'm still looking for that map myself."

There was obvious public good in revealing the location of the pipes, and frightened citizens were clamoring to know. "The public has a right to this information," said City Attorney Dennis Herrera—but did the public's right to know outweigh the potential harm in releasing the information? And who could make that call?

Lawyers advised us not to reveal the information, and some of my staff agreed. We had a lot of meetings and listened to people's concerns about the public-safety aspect. But after weighing the opinions on all sides, I decided that the information had to be released. Terrorists can find any number of targets to attack, from water reservoirs to subway trains to bridges to sporting venues. It makes no sense to create a climate of such abject fear that we feel compelled to hide any scrap of information that could conceivably be used to harm us.

This is just one example of the thousands of decisions that are made every day about which data are safe and appropriate to release. There are plenty of safeguards built in—departments, commissions, task forces—to assess what's safe and what's not. And these are conversations we must continue having, as there's no one-size-fits-all remedy.

In an interview on the tech blog *O'Reilly Radar,* New York City's Department of Information Technology and Telecommunications commissioner Carole Post put it this way: "We first and foremost are a steward of the data we hold, and so the concerns around privacy, confidentiality and public safety are definitely ones that need to be balanced against accessibility to the information." Yet at the same time, the day is coming when we'll share all our data by default, only holding back things that are public-safety concerns.

This is no longer a question of if but of when. It's inevitable. And the reality is, we may not even have the option to hold back some information. We've learned that the hard way, through WikiLeaks.

## WIKILEAKS AND THE END OF PRIVACY

Over the last year and a half, I've asked dozens of people what they think about the WikiLeaks phenomenon. When Julian Assange and his team began publishing reams of government information online—some of it top secret—he changed the entire dynamic for government officials. Cables and memos that were meant to be classified were suddenly out in the open for anyone to see. And there was no guarantee that private documents would ever be private again. This changed forever the way diplomacy had operated; no longer could officials count on the cloak of secrecy for what they were doing.

Was this an inevitable result of the Internet age? Will it continue? Does government simply have to accept that nothing is guaranteed to be private anymore? And is that ultimately a bad thing or a good thing?

I asked many people these questions, and on one point, everyone agreed: WikiLeaks is the new norm. No matter how safe we try to keep our data, there will always be ways for people to get hold of it—through hackers, spies, or simply people sympathetic to the WikiLeaks cause. Moving forward, we have no choice but to assume that all data might end up as public data, whether we like it or not.

Where people differ is on whether this is a good thing. President Clinton was wary, saying, "I think data is good. But the problem I had with the WikiLeaks thing was the almost unnecessary implication that, if you agree with what WikiLeaks did, is that no one who works for any level of government should ever be able to communicate confidentially with anyone else who works for that level of government unless they do it verbally, either face-to-face or by a cell-phone conversation that can't be intercepted. And I don't think that's right."

Arianna Huffington had this to say: "WikiLeaks was inevitable. It was bound to happen. Technology was going to make it much harder for governments to have any secrecy. But what WikiLeaks showed was, there's often a huge discrepancy between what government claims is happening and what is actually going on." And this, of course, is why we want open data in the first place—to shine a light on what our government is doing, to keep it honest, and to increase trust.

"The genie is out of the bottle," Sunlight's Ellen Miller told me. "If government isn't going to do transparency, we are going to do it to them." Or as Wim Elfrink put it, "WikiLeaks is fantastic. It's democracy."

I'm generally in favor of transparency, though I wouldn't go so far as Elfrink in saying WikiLeaks is fantastic. WikiLeaks makes our institutions naked, putting everything out there to be seen by whoever's looking. That can be good, as Stewart Brand says: "To some extent, excessive secrecy has been analyzed as the effort of an organism to hide its pathologies from itself." When you're naked, there's nowhere to hide anything. You're forced to be more open and honest than you otherwise might have been.

Yet there are consequences to complete transparency, too—in both diplomacy and governance. If you can't have completely honest conversations in e-mail, for fear that your words will go public and either be misinterpreted or undermine your cause, that's not helpful to anyone. I experienced this firsthand in 2006, when a front-page *San Francisco Chronicle* article criticized me for e-mails sent between me and Google's Larry Page and Sergey Brin. The e-mails themselves were benign, just arranging travel details and meeting times—but seeing excerpts from friendly e-mails between the mayor and two of the most prominent entrepreneurs in the Bay Area got people's hackles up.

That, unfortunately, had a chilling effect. With all of us anxious about being criticized, we cut back on our communication just at a point when we were discussing the implementation of free wi-fi throughout San Francisco—one of the projects I'd been fighting hard for as mayor. And I realized—as so many government officials have—that e-mail is a blessing and a curse. Sending and receiving e-mails creates the kind of "paper" trail that can easily be picked apart by critics.

After that 2006 incident, I cut back on using e-mail, a decision that certainly didn't help productivity. The truth is, if you can write in e-mails only things that you'd be happy to see on the front page of the local newspaper, you have to leave out a lot. That's what WikiLeaks has done: It has made government and diplomacy much more challenging and ultimately less honest, as people fear that their private communications might become public. It's governing in a reality-TV environment. But thanks to Julian Assange, that WikiLeaks environment is the one we live in now, so we have no choice but to adapt.

Is it appropriate for Assange and WikiLeaks to release this information? Is it safe? In the end, these questions don't matter. It is happening, and it's going to keep happening, and it's going to intensify. This is the beginning of the end of anonymity and hidden data. So instead of spending our time fighting it, we have to get out in front of it, to plan ahead for it.

And the same is true not only for government information and data, but also for *your* information and data. One of the biggest concerns about this new age of data has been protecting people's privacy. But is that even possible anymore? Or has the world changed so dramatically that privacy doesn't matter?

## WE ALL HAVE PAPARAZZI NOW

"There's no such thing as a private individual anymore," George Clooney told me one sunny afternoon in Los Angeles. I sat down with George, who knows a thing or two about being a public figure—and about politics—to ask him what he thought about the disconnect between people and politics in the age of technology.

"Now that everyone can get on Facebook, if you do something really stupid—you do something bigoted, or some dumb naked dance or whatever—you are no longer a private entity," George said. "You are a public person. . . . On Facebook, those images don't belong to you. They belong to Facebook. You're no longer afforded the same privacy laws. I think it's terrible, but that's another of those moments where you go walking full-face into it."

This is perhaps not surprising, coming from a man who famously declared that he'd "rather have a prostate exam on live television by a guy with very cold hands than have a Facebook page." But is his point of view extreme? I asked a number of other people what they thought about privacy. Almost everyone said the same thing: Privacy is dead.

As Jeremy Stoppelman, the founder of Yelp, put it, "In general, in the Facebook era, we're pretty much living in public. It used to be that only celebrities had to worry about paparazzi, but now everyone's got paparazzi." The message from Stoppelman and many others was the same: Worrying about privacy at this point is like worrying about how to stop a tsunami. You can't do it. You can only prepare as best you can for the consequences.

These days, your phone tracks your every movement. So does your car, if you have GPS. New cars will be coming out with Internet connectivity, and they'll all be connected to a traffic monitoring system, for better real-time traffic information. If you walk down the street in your city, you're photographed by innumerable cameras—at ATMs, outside banks, outside stores. Google Street View camera cars snap millions of photographs every day, some of them of people in compromising positions or embarrassing places. Traffic cameras snap photos of your car shooting through intersections. FasTrak toll-lane cameras snap your car and license tag as you're traveling down the highway.

There's no privacy left, even in your home. We now have smart meters that reveal when you turned your lights on and off. We'll soon have real-time pricing on video feeds. Someone will be tracking what you're watching, when you turned your lights off, when you turned your thermostat down to go to bed. When you Yelp, your phone tracks where you are and what you're searching for. When you read an article through Social Reader, it shows up in your Facebook feed. When you listen to music on Spotify, Facebook alerts all your friends. We've raced past the era of privacy. We're now in the era when we have to "learn to stop worrying and love the bomb."

Peter Schwartz, one of the first hackers in history—the main character in the 1983 movie *WarGames* was based on him—has an interesting take on all this, one I hadn't heard before. He believes that privacy was a relatively new phenomenon anyway, so we're just reverting back to the norm. "Privacy was an artifact of the early part of the last century," he told me. "In little towns, throughout history, there was no privacy—everybody knew everybody's business. You only got privacy when you moved into the city, where you lived entirely by yourself. You didn't know your neighbors in your apartment building, but you certainly did in your small town." This is a relatively recent phenomenon; in some ways, we've had very little true privacy in all of human history—only about a hundred years in which people were able to disappear into faceless urban anonymity. "But that's all gone," he says. "Now I can see my hot tub on Google Earth."

Schwartz has always been in the forefront of technology and connectivity, but that doesn't mean he embraces it without hesitation. "I prefer my privacy," he told me, "but I think [Marshall] McLuhan was right: We live in a global village. . . . Don't you assume that everything you say and do—someone is going to be able to find out?"

Guy Kawasaki, the former chief evangelist of Apple and the author of ten books on innovation and technology, seems bemused by all the fuss. "It's an emotional issue that for all intents and purposes is irrelevant," he said. "This whole Facebook thing—you click on LIKE, and then even if you're not signed in anymore, it knows where you are. But that's not a problem, assuming you didn't go straight from your Facebook page to a pedophile site." There's a simple solution to all the hand-wringing, he says. "My privacy policy is 'Don't do bad things.'"

Tech journalist Greg Ferenstein sees some good in the move to transparency. "We're not as perfect as we thought we were," he says. "We're also not as judgmental. The example I like to use is that the Internet is an experiment in a glass neighborhood. If you build a glass neighborhood, would everyone walk around covered up? Or do they do naked yoga? It turns out, they do naked yoga," he says. People are choosing to reveal all kinds of things, even though they know—or should know—that the information will be out there, visible to anyone, forever. But as Ferenstein notes, "If one person does naked yoga, he's an outcast. If everyone does naked yoga, it's a party."

George Clooney also believes that this new fishbowl existence will have some positive effects. "One benefit that's going to come from this is, scandal will become less and less," he told me. "There was a period of time when a game show almost brought down an entire network because of a little cheating," he said, referring to the infamous *Twenty-One* quiz show scandal that severely damaged NBC in the fifties. "Now that would just be a blip on the radar. We're able to forgive and forget such amazing scandals now. So perhaps the only good that comes out of this is, you're not able to use scandal anymore as a weapon. You know, there are reality-show stars who are famous for doing porn—and they're making millions of dollars now," he said. "Whether that's good or bad, what it really says is, scandal is huge but it only lasts for a minute. And then it doesn't stick."

## WE WANT OUR COOKIES

As someone who's seen much of his personal life displayed on the pages of newspapers and blogs, I'm not as bothered as some by the end of personal privacy. It's a price I've paid for being in public life. And as I learned while I was mayor, and now as lieutenant governor, the more information you put out there, the better off you are. The secret to surviving the loss of privacy as a politician is to push the envelope on it yourself: Get the information out there before someone else reports it about you, as that's the only way to control it. Just as with open data, sunlight is the best disinfectant.

Another benefit is that ending privacy means ending the anonymity that has spread hostility and hatred like a contagion throughout the Web. Wherever there's an opportunity for people to post comments anonymously, the discourse invariably sinks to the lowest common denominator of name-calling, insults, and flame wars. People become their worst selves. Civility falls by the wayside. When that layer of privacy is eliminated and people are forced to stand publicly behind what they say, civility returns.

Roger Ehrenberg suggests another benefit to loss of privacy. "Are most people aware of the implicit pact that they've made, with the trade-off of privacy on one end and security on the other? And when I mean security, I mean personal security and national security. In a world of infinite transparency and zero privacy, it's a lot safer." There's nowhere for those who would do ill to hide.

And there's another crucial point about privacy, which is that the millennial generation—people thirty and under—don't seem to care about it as much as those over thirty. They've grown up in a world where they've made trade-offs every day, setting up their browsers to accept cookies, submitting addresses and credit-card numbers online, and spending their entire adult lives on Facebook posting photos and intimate details of their lives.

As Daniel Lyons wrote in *Newsweek:*

Maybe it's a generational thing. People my age (nearly 50, a.k.a. "the olds" in blogosphere parlance) would probably rather part with a few bucks than with our personal information. Younger people don't have as much money, and don't care as much about privacy. So they're happy to go along with the deal being offered to them by Google and Facebook. What's happening is that our privacy has become a kind of currency. The genius of Google, Facebook and others is that they've created services that are so useful or entertaining that people will give up some privacy in order to use them. Now the trick is to get people to give up more—in effect, to keep raising the price of the service.

Recent studies back this up, showing growing concern for millennials with regard to privacy. Euro RSCG Worldwide's *Prosumer Report* released a study called *This Digital Life,* which stated six out of every ten people surveyed believed people should stop sharing so much information. And millennials essentially confirmed that they were the ones doing a lot of that sharing; 66 percent of them agreed with the statement "Young people today have no sense of personal privacy; they're willing to post anything and everything about their lives online."

According to a study released by Aimia, a company that builds and runs brand-loyalty programs, millennials are much less concerned about privacy when taking part in loyalty programs. In other words, young people are more than willing to share their personal information if it means getting discounts and rewards. They are the choice generation—a generation that has never known a world without the innumerable commercial, educational, and entertainment options granted by the Internet.

For millennials, the notion of going back to a world where privacy reigns is unthinkable. "Think of a world with [Internet] cookies," Ehrenberg says, "I'm getting pushed ads, and those ads have absolutely no contextual relevance. Do people want that? No, we kind of had that before—that was called the Web '95—and it didn't work very well. There was zero monetization. . . . Now when I see ads, they're starting to get pretty darn good. And when I get offers e-mailed to me, they're getting better and better and better. And you know what I say? That's cool. That's OK. I'm fine with that." And so, it seems, are the digital natives who have never known another, more private, way of life.

I have a three-year-old daughter, and when she grabs my iPad and starts swiping through, playing games and looking at pictures and changing the music, it's absolutely clear that new generations see the world completely differently than my generation does. This is our future customer base; these are our future constituents. And the future is happening now.

# FOUR

# There's an App for That

IN LATE DECEMBER 2006, a guy named Michal Migurski was laid up with a bad back. The technical director for Stamen Design, a Web design and data-visualization studio, Mike had two weeks off for the holidays. Normally, he'd have been out and about, but his back was hurting too much to go anywhere.

Mike stayed home, messing around at a raised computer desk because he couldn't sit without pain. With two weeks to kill, he found himself thinking, *How can I spend this time productively?* He lived in Oakland, California, which has a reputation for high crime rates, so he decided to start poking around the data on Oakland's official Crime-Watch Web site. He was dismayed at what he found.

"Oakland had the bare minimum necessary to show people what crimes were happening," he said. "What they had was something probably commissioned in the late nineties or so—that's what it looked like. It was the sort of system where you had to know what you were looking for before it would tell you anything. . . . It gives you exactly what you ask for, nothing more and nothing less."

Mike knew there had to be more data out there and a better way to present it. He had followed the work of a Web developer named Adrian Holovaty, who in 2005 created a site called ChicagoCrime.org (now part of Chicago's EveryBlock site)—a mash-up of Chicago's official crime data with Google Maps. Holovaty, who calls what he does journalism via computer programming, was one of the first to use Google Maps in this way, and his work helped lead to the creation of the Google Maps API (application programming interface)—a platform for creating all kinds of new mapping tools.

"I was interested to see if this was an experiment that was repeatable in other places," Mike recalled. "So I looked at how [Holovaty] had done his work, and the resources he had available to him in Chicago weren't available in Oakland," because of how poorly designed the CrimeWatch site was. The process of getting usable data for Oakland was "really painful and really time-consuming," said Migurski, because Chicago offered addresses and text, but Oakland didn't.

Oakland's data wasn't findable or standardized, making it all but useless to the average person. The only way to get it was to create a sophisticated data-scraping tool, which would automatically pull certain types of data from the CrimeWatch Web site. Mike was skilled enough to do it, though he knew the Oakland authorities might not like the idea, because it would eat up bandwidth and slow down their Web site.

What to do? Because Oakland's government offices were shut down for a couple of days over Christmas, there was no one to ask. So Mike decided just to forge ahead. "There's a certain ethos of asking for forgiveness rather than trying to get permission," he said, smiling. "I figured that one way to get the city's attention was to just shake the data out of the site, rather than ask whether it would be possible to shake the data out of the site."

Mike spent two weeks perfecting a data-scraping tool, which painstakingly pulled out relevant data from the scattered mass of information on the CrimeWatch site. Initially, he saw this task primarily as a technical puzzle he wanted to solve. Then he became obsessed with getting it done before his break ended. He didn't want the Oakland authorities to shut down his ability to scrape the data, so he automated the tool to do it overnight, when no one was likely to notice or be bothered by it. "This wasn't just a one-time process," Mike said. "It would pull out this data every night—a batch of fresh crime."

At first, no one in the Oakland government noticed. Mike's tool collected data every night, building up his new database. He went back to work at Stamen after the holiday break and did some internal experiments with his new data, but now he could only work on it part time. "It kind of cooked along on the back burner for a long time," he said.

Then in August 2007, an investigative journalist named Chauncey Bailey Jr. was shot to death just a few blocks from Mike's house. Bailey's murder became a national story—and it galvanized Mike to take his new crime site public.

"Mike lived in Oakland, so he took it personally," said his Stamen colleague Shawn Allen. "He wanted to figure out a way to allow people to engage with crime in a more direct way. When [Bailey] was killed, we decided to push it out into the world."

Mike immediately ramped up work on the project, which he dubbed Crimespotting, using Oakland's crime data to build an easy-to-use interactive site for seeing where crimes have been committed. When they pushed it live, Allen said, "It was an immediate smash. It allows you to create Excel spreadsheets [showing where crimes have happened], and we got e-mails from people saying they were going to the police station with these spreadsheets, saying, 'What's going on with this?'" People could see very clearly when crime was spiking in their neighborhoods, and they wanted answers.

"It was a total inversion of the usual relationship, where cops come around to say, 'Things have been happening in your neighborhood,'" said Allen. With Mike Migurski's tool, people suddenly knew as much as the Oakland police did—all because one guy started messing around in his spare time, digging up important data and figuring out how to make it useful.

## LEARNING TO ACCEPT A FREE GIFT

I love the story of Crimespotting, as it perfectly illustrates why data—and what we do with it—is so important. Mike Migurski uncovered data that was hidden, and he created a way for people to understand it. And he did this not because he wanted to get paid, because he had a bone to pick, or because he wanted to embarrass anyone. He did it because he was an ordinary guy who cared what was going on in his city.

Now let's imagine that the city of Oakland had decided they wanted to build the Crimespotting tool themselves. They probably don't have a Stamen-level Web design team on the city payroll, so they'd need to outsource the job. This usually consists of sending out a request for proposals, accepting bids over a period of months, and then choosing a contractor to fulfill the project. The cost might reach into the hundreds of thousands of dollars, and the end product may or may not have been as good as what Mike and his colleagues produced.

Essentially, Oakland got a free gift from a motivated citizen—one who was uniquely equipped to take available data and make it useful, which is the ideal of the open-data movement. And yet . . . they weren't happy about it. A few months after it launched, according to Migurski, Oakland tried to shut Crimespotting down, by interfering with the data scraping that provided the site's information.

"The IT department of the city of Oakland noticed what we'd been doing and closed us down," Mike said. "The first response we got wasn't even a direct response. It was just, you know, they saw the site, they presumably looked into their server logs to try to figure out where this data was coming from, found us, and closed us off. Their reasoning was that they felt we were placing an undue burden on their system resources. We didn't think we were."

Just as my intern John Hewitt discovered when he tried to migrate our office's data to the cloud, government IT departments are skittish in the face of new technological developments. Migurski tried to sidestep the Oakland officials' concerns, continuing to scrape data only at night, when hardly anyone else would be using the CrimeWatch site. But the city still objected.

"This is where our decision to talk to them only after it was worth their attention kind of worked out," Migurski said. "Because at this point there was a Web site, there was a bit of pressure where we could tell people, 'Oh, the city's shutting us down.' That put a little bit of pressure on them. I don't want to make it sound more adversarial than it was, but we definitely got their attention." Once people had seen what it was like to have easy, visual access to crime reports, they didn't want to lose it.

Of course, if Oakland simply worked with Mike and his team—say, by providing the data directly rather than forcing them to scrape it off the official Web site every night, that would solve everything. And fortunately that is what ended up happening. City officials eventually realized that Oakland's citizens wanted the service Crimespotting provided, so they agreed to make the data available.

"We talked about different ways they could get us the data," said Migurski. "Now, once per night, there's some kind of automated process in the city's IT infrastructure that posts a simple spreadsheet to the Web, with block-level crime information." A win-win-win situation: The city provides useful data, the Crimespotting team puts it in usable form, people can track crime in their areas, and police can get a clearer picture of crime trends and respond to them accordingly. No downside for anyone—except criminals.

As a postscript, Migurski's company, Stamen, ended up getting its own benefits from Crimespotting. The mapping design that the team created became a base map for another project, and eventually all of their mapping projects. "At first it was an excuse to build some new technology," said Shawn Allen. "But other projects fed into that." So the time the team spent developing this free Web site for the city actually turned out to be a valuable investment for Stamen.

## THE COGNITIVE SURPLUS

That's a wonderful story, I can hear you saying, but let's get real. How many people would do what Mike Migurski did? How many people would spend so many hours working for free? Wasn't Crimespotting just an unusual case?

Clay Shirky doesn't think so. In 2010, Shirky released a book called *Cognitive Surplus: Creativity and Generosity in a Connected Age*. In it, he argued that in today's industrialized world, we have all kinds of free time now that we no longer have to hunt, gather, harvest, hand-wash our clothes, and all those other time-consuming activities people have historically been burdened with.

Yet the free time we've gained became "something to be used up rather than used," as Shirky put it in a *Wired* magazine interview, "especially in postwar America, with the rise of suburbanization and long commutes. Suddenly we no longer lived in tight-knit communities and therefore we spent less time interacting face-to-face. As a result, we ended up spending the bulk of our free time watching television."

Shirky estimates that a person born in 1960 has watched about fifty thousand hours of television. "But once we stop thinking of all that time as individual minutes to be whiled away and start thinking of it as a social asset that can be harnessed, it all looks very different," he said. "The buildup of this free time among the world's educated population—maybe a trillion hours per year—is a new resource." Shirky has dubbed this the cognitive surplus, and he believes it has the potential to change how we live and work.

To illustrate his point, Shirky refers to the creation of Wikipedia, the online encyclopedia written and edited entirely by volunteers. By his calculations, Wikipedia represents about 100 million hours of labor. This is a tremendous investment of human resources—all of it unpaid. Yet Americans watch 200 billion hours of television every single year. So that seemingly huge time investment in Wikipedia is actually a mere 0.05 percent of the time we spend every single year watching television.

We obviously have a lot more time than we think we do. But are people really inclined to spend their spare hours working for free? Doesn't that go against human nature, especially in a country like the United States, where everything and everyone has its price?

Daniel Pink, an editor at *Wired* and the author of *Drive: The Surprising Truth About What Motivates Us,* says people will happily work for free. He illustrates his point in the same *Wired* interview with Shirky:

Think about open source software in general—whether it's Linux or Apache. Suppose I'd gone to an economist or management consultant

25 years ago and said, "I've got a cool new business model for making software. Here's how it works: A bunch of intrinsically motivated people around the world get together to do technically sophisticated stuff for no pay. And then after working really hard, they give away their product for free. Trust me: It's going to be huge."

Who would ever have thought people would work so hard to create an amazingly valuable product—and then give it away? Yet that's exactly what we've seen, time and again, in the Internet age.

Want to blog? Here's some free software you can use to get started. Want to post hundreds of photos and find old friends with the click of a button? Here's a free site called Facebook that will let you do it. Want to call your friend in Bulgaria for free, via your computer? Here's a service called Skype that makes it possible. And all these products and services are building value with every new customer they add.

In February 2012, when Facebook announced its planned initial public offering (IPO), people marveled at its $94 billion valuation (on the day of the IPO, which was disrupted by a technical glitch at the NASDAQ stock exchange, the company's valuation was more than $100 billion). For a company that had existed only eight years and that charged its customers nothing, these felt like astronomical sums of money. But what made it even more extraordinary was a fact many analysts overlooked. At the time of its IPO, Facebook's total number of employees was about 3,200. In comparison, Amazon, with a market capitalization of about $82 billion, had 56,000 employees. And McDonald's, with a market capitalization of about $101 billion—about the same as Facebook's—had *1.7 million* employees. Facebook had the fewest number of employees for any company approaching its size, by far.

Why? Because Facebook's users, not its employees, produce its content. Facebook may have had only 3,200 or so paid employees, but as 2012 came to a close, it had approximately a billion users. The company let those users do for themselves what it could never have done profitably itself: create billions of pages of content. And we're seeing this model more and more—think of newspaper Web sites posting readers' photos and eyewitness accounts, or the *Huffington Post* parlaying unpaid blog posts into a $315 million business.

Here's another example: Apple's App Store was launched in June 2008. Within two years, it carried more than 225,000 apps—from games and business tools to travel aids and social networking—and users had made *4 billion* downloads from the store to their devices. By June 2010, the average iPhone user was spending $80 on apps, about 70 percent of which goes to the app designer, Apple taking the rest.

So Apple makes millions of dollars annually by selling apps that other people have created for it. Simply by offering an open API— a platform on which people can build apps easily—Apple created immense value not only for itself, but also for its customers. This, too, is a new way of doing things—one that the world of business has quickly embraced. Any company that refuses to let consumers create their own content and apps will fall behind in this brave new marketplace.

We in government have to take advantage of this truth and make it not only possible but easy for people to create things—Web sites, apps, software—with the data we've collected. We need to free our data, open up government APIs, and create our own apps stores modeled after the Apple apps experience. We have to learn, as these multibillion-dollar companies have, to let others do the work.

# NOT SO GREAT MOMENTS IN TECHNOLOGY AND GOVERNMENT

Here's another reason we should be outsourcing technology: Government, when it tries to handle tech issues itself, tends to get in way over its head. A perfect example of this was the Terry Childs incident, which happened toward the end of my second term as mayor. It was like a Keystone Kops episode, a cautionary tale if ever there was one.

Terry Childs was a forty-three-year-old network engineer for the city of San Francisco. He worked on our fiber-optic network, called FiberWAN, which handled crucial government data, such as e-mail, legal documents, and payroll. By most accounts, he was a diligent and talented employee, and he seemed dedicated to making sure our systems ran safely.

Childs spent hours trying to perfect our FiberWAN system, upgrading equipment and installing firewalls. He had a high opinion of his own skills, even applying to get a copyright for the "technical artistry" he brought to the network. He unilaterally decided when to add hardware to the system, hooking up new computer equipment down at the city's Department of Technology. Eventually it became apparent that he was the only person who knew all the codes and passwords to operate the system.

This was obviously not the ideal operating protocol, but it might not have been a catastrophe—except for the fact that in the summer of 2008, Childs was reassigned, and when he was instructed to hand over the password he had created for FiberWAN, he refused.

Just like that, one man now held the city's most valuable data hostage. No one could get into the FiberWAN without that password—e-mails were inaccessible, payroll couldn't go out, and documents were under virtual lock and key. Childs had, under the noses of everyone, built a system that he could choke off at will.

Childs holed up at his home, refusing to tell anyone the password, as the local media ran wild with the story. Some commenters to local media Web site SFGate.com suggested that we waterboard him, while others saw him as some kind of folk hero. We had no choice but to try to compel him to give up the password, so the police arrested Childs on a charge of felony computer tampering and put him in jail. But he still wouldn't give up the code.

The city was in crisis. We had to have that code! We spent at least a million dollars, including hiring a team at Cisco Systems, to crack the code, but they couldn't do it. Days went by, and the story went national. How could this be—how could one man hold an entire city hostage, and what did that portend for the rest of us in this new technological age?

In the midst of all this, I was scheduled to get married in Montana. I knew that leaving the city with this problem unresolved—even for my own wedding—would unleash a torrent of criticism. So when Childs's attorney said Childs would be willing to talk to me, as long as I came by myself and there was no media fanfare, I jumped at the chance. Eight days after Childs was arrested, I went to the jail in secret, to ask him face-to-face for the code.

"Listen, Terry," I said. "I'm going to lay it out here for you. I'm not going to moralize. I'm getting married in a few days, and I'm desperate. The city needs the code. Please." I was as honest as I could be, asking him to give me the code as a favor, if nothing else. And he responded.

Childs said he didn't trust his bosses or colleagues, but at that moment, he trusted me. He wrote down the code—all twenty-eight numbers and letters of it—and handed it over. And although some feared that this might be a booby trap set by Childs, a code that would self-destruct the entire system, I believed he had played it straight. And he had. The code unlocked the FiberWAN system, and order was finally restored.

Can you imagine anything similar happening at a company like Oracle, Microsoft, Twitter, or Yelp? This may be an extreme case, but the lesson is clear: Technology is not the government's core competency. In government service, there tend to be a few people who are empowered and entrusted with an extraordinary amount of influence, usually based on seniority. Terry Childs was a brilliant technologist who cowed his colleagues into allowing him to amass total control over a critical city resource. No one in his department really knew what he was doing with all those new modems and servers, and we found out only when it was too late.

We just don't have the resources in government to get the numbers and quality of tech employees we need. In fact, tech is usually the first place that funding gets cut. When you're looking for programs to trim to satisfy a shrinking budget, what goes first? Police? Firefighters? Senior meals? Of course not. You cut costs that no one will protest. And every year, the first place that gets whacked is IT.

That's how we end up with failed projects like the brand-new computer system for CalPERS, the California Public Employees' Retirement System, which was intended to consolidate forty-nine old data systems into one streamlined system. Unfortunately, the project was completed two years late, cost a half-billion dollars—nearly twice the original estimate—and resulted in even worse services, with longer backlogs than before it was implemented.

In 2001, California governor Gray Davis signed a $95 million contract with Oracle for significant IT upgrades. A huge scandal ensued, mostly because it was a no-bid contract and Davis received a $25,000 check toward his reelection campaign from Oracle just days later. But the real scandal was that the contract was a boondoggle—Oracle's upgrade was supposed to save the state about $111 million above the contract's cost (if the state exercised an option for additional maintenance). But instead, an audit committee found that the state would in fact spend almost $6 million more on Oracle database licenses and maintenance if it exercised that option and almost $41 million more if it didn't.

How could this happen? It happened because no one on the government side had enough knowledge to properly assess what Oracle was promising and whether it made sense. It happened because government will never be able to lure the kind of programming talent it needs.

## "PEOPLE WILL DO IT . . . BECAUSE IT'S COOL"

"Finding great engineers is really difficult," Yelp cofounder Jeremy Stoppelman told me. "The hot tech companies in the Valley—we'll all complain until your ears bleed about how we can't hire the best engineers. How can city government get a team of badass engineers to work on problems if Google or Facebook or Yelp can't hire them?" With no stock options, no hype, and only the promise of slow, steady advance within its civil-service ranks, government has very little to offer a talented young programmer.

We have to offer the next best thing, an open platform for people to experiment, to create and distribute government apps. Our problems are so big and so expensive that we can't afford to buy solutions. But replicating Apple's model for the App Store is the antidote: Government doesn't have to come up with new killer features on its own. It has to step aside and let others come up with them.

"When you put the data you possibly have out there, into the public domain, making it accessible to any creative mind, really smart people will pick it up and play with it," says Stoppelman. "People will do it for no more serious reason than because it's cool." Government just has to be open, move quickly, and make things simple for those who can help it.

But as we know, government doesn't think that way. It's not designed to. As James Q. Wilson wrote in his influential 1989 book, *Bureaucracy:*

> Government has to be slower, has to safeguard process. . . . It is not hyperbole to say that constitutional order is animated by a desire to make government inefficient. . . . Americans distrust anyone who wields power and sought to prevent abuse by surrounding all power-wielders with constitutional checks and laws.

By its very nature, American government wants to move slowly. In many ways, that's a good thing; our steady, stable 235-year-old system has proven itself both strong and durable. But with the advent of the digital age, there's a natural tension between the new, fast-moving tech world and government. Stewart Brand says it's the difference between those who want to solve problems and those who want to debate them. "How many engineers do you know who are running for public office?" Brand asked me, before answering the question himself—"Almost none." In fact, as of February 2012, according to the *New York Times*, the 435-member House of Representatives had "one physicist, one

THERE'S AN APP FOR THAT

chemist, one microbiologist, six engineers, and nearly two dozen representatives with medical training." A large proportion of people who run for public office are lawyers. And the way lawyers approach problems, notes Brand, is very different from the way engineers do.

"When problem solvers come up against government, they feel it's an institution not interested in solving problems," he says simply. "It's interested in *debating* problems."

He uses Apple cofounders Steve Wozniak and Steve Jobs as an example. "At the same time that Woz and Jobs were doing their thing, across the bay at Berkeley, it was still 'Power to the People!'" Brand said. "These guys demanded nothing, protested nothing. They just built things that *actually* gave people power. Demanding stuff doesn't do much. It does more than nothing, but building the workarounds for the problem, noisily or quietly, actually can make the problem go away. "This is the opposite of a romantic approach to government issues," he concludes. "It's an engineering approach." And there just aren't many people within government who subscribe to that approach.

So what to do? We obviously don't have the money, the skilled programmers, or the engineering mind-set within government to address our problems in the age of technology. Once again, we don't have to. We simply have to make it possible for people *outside* government to help us fix them. We have to think of government as a convener. A concierge, if you will—a customer-service organization.

## CODE FOR AMERICA

Jennifer Pahlka has spent a lot of time thinking about how to bridge the gap between government and technology. She's been in tech media for more than fifteen years, running the Game Developers Conference and *Game Developer* magazine for nearly a decade and then heading up the Web 2.0 summit for TechWeb. She also helped launch the first Gov 2.0 summit in 2009—and that's when she had her epiphany.

Pahlka and Tim O'Reilly, the visionary behind Web 2.0, were having an ongoing conversation about how to get more tech people involved in government. She had a notion that getting people involved at the city level was the way to go, but she couldn't figure out how to lure people away from potentially lucrative opportunities in the private sector. It was a puzzle she couldn't crack, until one fateful day in Arizona.

"I was on vacation with my family," she told me, "and this guy came to visit. He had done Teach For America and was talking about his experience, and suddenly I thought, *That's how you get people to do it.* Not for money, but for love. People will do stuff if they feel like they're serving their country. It was right then and there: Code for America."

Pahlka quit her job and founded Code for America, a nonprofit that provides tech-savvy fellows to city governments for short-term projects. Code for America identifies specific government problems that need Web-based solutions; then it matches them with teams of fellows—Web developers and designers—who decamp to each city to solve the problem. "It's a mash-up of Teach For America, the Peace Corps, and Y Combinator," she told me.

"My first big job was developing this gaming conference," said Pahlka. "PlayStation, Wii—they live and die by the third-party developer community that's attached to them. Those tech evangelists—that's who you need in city government." If government could attract the kind of developer community that has added so much value to gaming, there's no telling how much technology in governance could be improved. "This is the space, this is the opportunity—come create something!" enthused Pahlka. "It's all the same levers. We can play those same cards to get people involved."

This kind of innovation and leadership is exactly what we need to begin solving the problems of government. Just as Pahlka surmised, people were excited to spend six months helping to make government better. Code for America teams have created all kinds of useful tools, including a Web site in Boston that maps snowbound fire hydrants, so residents can "adopt" them and make sure they're functional throughout the winter, and a program that tracks school buses using GPS, so parents know when the buses are running late. These projects might never have been created without the CfA teams. And Pahlka gave me more examples of ways CfA projects have enhanced the cultural and social lives of cities.

"Our Philadelphia team found this data set of all the murals—and there are many beautiful murals—in Philadelphia," she told me. "They mapped them and created a mobile app that will take you on a walking tour of all the really cool public art in Philadelphia. It illustrates a couple of things about our model: That's not something you could probably have gotten a grant to do, because you didn't know it was there! It's an emergent outcome of having really smart, technically savvy people who get that this is very easy to do. . . . And the other thing it illustrates about our program is that this shouldn't just be in Philly; it should be everywhere. So San Francisco is the second place we've brought it to."

I went downtown to check out the San Francisco team at work and found a posse of hackers, all excited about doing this cool thing for their city. But as it turned out, they'd had to do some convincing to get city officials to release the data about murals. Why? Because the officials were embarrassed about the state the data was in.

"The data was really scary," Pahlka told me with a laugh. "On spreadsheets, on paper—it took [our team] a while to clean it up. . . . They kept saying, 'It's OK that your data's not in good shape! It's fine! This is the value that will come out of it.' They have the perspective to say, 'The data was in bad shape in Philly, too. Don't be ashamed.'"

The real beauty of the project, though, is what happened next. Because San Francisco's data wasn't complete, the team had to find another way to map where all the public art was. So they decided to crowdsource. They called for a public art scavenger hunt, inviting people to walk around the city and take note of where the murals were, then report back to the team so they could be included in the walking-tour app.

Can you imagine government doing that? You'd need a team of six! You'd need a project manager! It would cost thousands of dollars and take months, if not years, to make it a reality. But as we spoke, Pahlka showed me the app—as she was testing it, dots started to appear in more and more places on the map as people reported where the art was. "What we hope will happen is that stuff like art maps will gain more users and contributors," said Pahlka. "Or that this platform will encourage citizens to solve problems on their own."

That alone is reason to support Code for America, but Pahlka sees other benefits, too. "The second level of outcomes," she said, "are what have fellows learned from working with city government, and what have city governments learned from us? We hope there are significant outcomes on both sides—it's not a one-way thing. We want to see our fellows graduate and go on to leadership positions that are impacted by their deep civic engagement. We hope some will become CIOs of cities or go on and do startups with a civic angle."

"And the third level outcome," she concluded, "is increasing the notion that you can Code for America, whatever that might mean for you. Just this idea that people want to get involved . . . that you want to be on the right end of a trend."

There is much good to be gained from projects like Code for America—creating new, useful apps for cities, increasing public engagement, instilling a more entrepreneurial vibe into city governments, and educating city officials that opening up data is the wave of the future. Unfortunately, some cities have openly rejected that idea.

"D.C. kicked us out in February, on the street in twenty-degree weather," Pahlka told me. "Literally, they escorted our fellows from the building, by security, on their very first day. Their general counsel walked up to them as they were getting ready to go to lunch and said, 'You need to leave the building,'" Pahlka told me. The reason? Code for America's D.C. contract had been signed under Mayor Adrian Fenty's administration. But when they started, in February, Vincent Gray had been sworn in as the new mayor. Gray's administration apparently decided that the Code for America contract was a relic of the Fenty era. "So now we know," Pahlka said with a weary smile, "not to contract with any cities that have elections coming up."

But if we are to continue to reap the benefits of fantastic programs like Code for America, city governments must be educated to let them come in and help, no matter how difficult, embarrassing, or politically risky that might feel. And that includes embracing the "white-hat hackers" who are trying, with every skill at their disposal, to improve our government systems.

## WHITE-HAT HACKERS

On the day I sat with Stewart Brand in his Sausalito office, he told me about the early days of white-hat hackers.

"The hackers conference we put together in '83 or '84," he said, "with Steve Wozniak and various people from MIT . . . it was one of those deals where we went around the room and said, 'What's your goal?' And Richard Stallman got up and said, 'I want free software for everybody.'" At the time, with personal computers just starting to penetrate the consumer market, software was ballooning into a hugely lucrative business. But these guys wanted it to be free, an idea that would have sounded crazy to anyone not in that room.

"And we did it!" Brand said with a smile. "Open-source software was brought into existence." The hackers knew what was best, even though it went against the prevailing wisdom, and they made it happen for the benefit of us all. Brand, who calls himself a metahacker, says, "I'm in education, and my goal is to make more of us. . . . The idea behind the *Whole Earth Catalog* was access to tools, power to the people." For Brand, white-hat hacking is a natural outgrowth of that power shift.

Despite the negative connotation of the word *hacker,* Brand defines white-hat hackers as people who are "benevolent fixers of things that are broken or not as good as they could be." And society, he says, "is in the process of making itself more hackable—in a good way—ideally, more hackable by benevolent hackers rather than the assholes." In other words, in this more open era, we have to be prepared for the incursions that will inevitably come. Instead of doing business as usual, expecting that our systems and data are impregnable, we have to play differently.

He gave me an example. "iGEM [the annual International Genetically Engineered Machine Foundation conference] is a gathering of nearly two hundred student teams from all over the world, twenty-six countries, that meet every fall at MIT. They create new microorganisms—they're undergraduates doing world-class genetic engineering of microbes." This is exciting from an educational perspective, but frightening from a law-enforcement one because of the ongoing threat of bioterrorism. In the past, the FBI might have tried to shut it down—as Brand says of his early *Whole Earth Catalog* period, "I remember days when they'd show up at hacker meetings, like we were all criminals"—but now it's taking a different approach.

"There's an FBI guy who shows up at iGEM meetings and at bio-hackers meetings," Brand told me. "His card says his name and FBI—WEAPONS OF MASS DESTRUCTION. . . . So he shows up and says, 'I think what you people are doing is fabulous; for undergraduates to be doing this level of work is extraordinary. I'm from the government and I'm here to help. Here's my phone number. If anyone sees problematic stuff going on, it's going to be you characters. And I want you . . . to give me a call, send me an e-mail, send me a link, if you see anything weird going on.'" Instead of antagonizing the biohackers, this FBI agent works with them, ending up with more information than he'd have had otherwise—a win-win.

In cities throughout the country, hackathons are redefining the meaning of civic engagement. Programmers, designers, developers, and data crunchers gather together for a finite period—say, forty-eight hours or a week—to try to solve some of the city's problems. Over sandwiches and sodas, in marathon sessions of coding and design, people apply their skills for no other reason than to make their cities better.

In San Francisco, the Gray Area Foundation for the Arts (GAFFTA) sponsored the Summer of Smart—a three-month program of hackathons and other events aimed at getting people involved in the tech side of governance. A grand experiment that brought together artists, coders, activists, and designers to create apps for the city, the Summer of Smart led to random acts of hacking all over the city, as people thought up new ways to better civic systems.

Over the course of several forty-eight-hour hackathons, people developed ideas like hyperlocal sites for organizing volunteers, interactive tools for showing residents how their tax dollars had improved their neighborhoods, a smartphone app to help people carpool or bikepool to events . . . and on and on. The creative spirit unleashed by these marathon hacking sessions has spread throughout the city, encouraging others to dream up their own apps and services.

Peter Hirshberg, an entrepreneur and tech blogger who also serves as chairman of GAFFTA, told me about one particularly elegant hack on a system that desperately needed an upgrade. A woman who was an intern at Muni, San Francisco's Municipal Transportation Agency, showed up at a hackathon weekend. "She said, 'You know, citizens know where the bus is, but if you go ask an employee who works for Muni, they have a clipboard and a schedule; they don't use open data, they use walkie-talkies. So if there's a problem, they don't know,'" said Hirshberg. And it was true—in one of the most technologically advanced cities in the United States, we still had people standing on street corners with clipboards, marking when the Muni trains went by.

It was an absurd situation, and this intern knew it. "So she led a team that build this iPad app that replaces the clipboard, that actually clues the Muni guys in on these citizens' reports," said Hirshberg. She took it upon herself to build this tool, just because she could. Everyone loved it—except the *San Francisco Chronicle*, which took the opportunity to excoriate everyone who works at Muni for not coming up with the idea sooner. The tone of the article, as Hirshberg put it, was "Hackers 1, City 0."

Well, what I'd like to see is "Hackers 10,000, City 0." This is the perfect example of how the government can do best by simply getting out of the way (despite the fact that San Francisco's budget crunch means the city hasn't yet bought the iPads needed to fully implement the app). Like Mike Migurski's Crimespotting, the Muni iPad app shows what useful tools people can build when the government (a) opens up its data and (b) gets the hell out of the way.

# FIVE

# It's the Platform, Stupid

IN 2008, as I started my second term as San Francisco mayor, I was dismayed at how far behind we still were technologically. Police cars weren't equipped for e-mail. City Web sites weren't set up to take meaningful feedback online. We were surrounded by some of the best and brightest minds in technology, but we were still operating as though we were stuck in a time warp. A 2008 report on the city's police district station boundaries summed up the dismal state of technology in the SFPD:

> Technology is extremely limited at every station. . . . Officers are not afforded the ability to use the Internet, hampering their ability to conduct research or correspond by email with other law enforcement personnel, City departments and citizens. . . . While there are some newer computers, most of the computers are older models. At this point only Administrators have PDA's and department-issued cell phones. Officers are so desperate for this type of technology that some have resorted to using personal equipment to perform their jobs.

And the situation wasn't much better for citizens trying to communicate with us. At the time, the most efficient way was through our 311 service. Three-one-one was the phone number we set up for nonemergency calls from citizens: If a tree falls and blocks your street, call 311. If someone leaves a mattress on your curb, call 311. If a streetlight is out, call 311. It's the catchall government response service. So it would have been tremendously useful to have crunchable reports on what citizens were calling about, to identify patterns of problems. But we didn't. Instead, when I asked for 311 reports, I got handed stacks of PDF printouts.

People in the tech community have a phrase to describe PDF files: "where data goes to die." PDF, Adobe's portable document format, is great for sending documents electronically, but terrible if you actually want to do anything useful with those documents. Without permission built in by the file's creator, you can't mark them up or change them, and it's impossible to do more than a basic word or phrase search or to crunch their data. PDF is a horse and buggy in a racecar world.

I hired a former Voice of America reporter named Brian Purchia as my new media director and asked him if he could figure out how to fix this problem. That was the beginning of a two-year period in which we transformed our city government. We started digitizing, mashing up, and opening up everything we possibly could—far beyond what I had initially imagined when I brought Brian in.

We launched an EcoFinder app for the iPhone, so residents could easily find out where to recycle. We launched DataSF.org, so people could find government data online. We launched an official city apps store, to promote the apps people were creating for use with city data. We launched 311 for Twitter, becoming the first city where people could tweet their problems to city government—and get answers. And it all started, as Brian likes to say, with that single PDF sheet.

But in March 2010, our team really outdid itself. Together with the Obama administration, we launched Open 311, the first national API in government history. For the first time, people could communicate collaboratively, in real time, about things going on in their streets, neighborhoods, and cities. When we announced the initiative, I noted that we were the first city "to actually combine this new two-way communication technology with a 311 call center." One-way is dead; two-way is the future.

Vivek Kundra came to San Francisco, joining Twitter cofounder Biz Stone and my CTO, Chris Vein, for the launch. This is how he described it in his "Open 311" post in the Open Government Initiative section of the White House blog:

> Too often, people grumble that their complaints about government— be it city, county, state, or federal—get swallowed by the bureaucracy. Open 311 is an answer to that problem, placing the role of service evaluator and service dispatcher in the power of citizens' hands. Through this approach, new web applications can mash publicly available, real-time data from the cities to allow people to track the status of repairs or improvements, while also allowing them to make new requests for services. . . .

But the best thing was, we could get other cities on board and share it with them. We launched Open 311 with the support of cities such as Portland, Los Angeles, and Boston, and though I will admit that I do like being first, I was excited for all these cities to launch too. As I wrote in a blog post on Mashable.com, "We want every major city to join this effort. . . . The more cities behind this effort, the better for city budgets, citizens, and developers throughout the nation."

That's the beauty of an open API—any city can adopt it and then use apps and technology there as well. The more we can share, the better off we are. This is not a usual hallmark of government, but it should be. Why should each city have to invent the wheel all by itself? Doesn't it just make sense that, especially in this age when technology is changing so quickly, we should all share what we learn along the way?

That's why, in 2010, I launched PolicySF.org—a Web site that made available everything we were learning and developing in San Francisco. We posted "policy toolkits"—full packets of information on our initiatives, from universal health care to open data, so any city that was interested could replicate what we'd done. At the launch, I called it "a one-stop destination for idea sharing and collaboration."

If someone in Tulsa city government liked our health-care system, they could find out everything about it—all the original documents, the press clippings, the legislation, the legalese, the city attorney opinions, the people's feedback. Anyone could see at a glance what the roadblocks were, who threw them up, and how we got around them—nothing hidden, nothing secret, just a blueprint for how to get the thing done.

The future is sharing—open data, open participation, open source, open everything. And it must happen at every level. People have already learned to share in their personal lives—through Yelp reviews, YouTube videos, tweets, and Facebook posts. Governments have started to share with the people through open data, open calendars, open APIs. And now governments must learn to share with each other through communication and collaboration. All of this sharing results in the strengthening of our commonwealth.

## THE LEGACY BURDEN

Tim O'Reilly is the chief evangelist of the government-as-platform movement. "First, a lot of us were talking about the Web as platform," he told me. "Treating the Internet as a platform distinguished the sites that survived the dot-com bust from those that failed. But then I realized that many of those ideas could be translated to government as platform, and that got everybody really excited.

"The key idea is this," he said. "The best way for government to operate is to figure out what kinds of things are enablers of society and then make investments in those things. The same way that Apple figured out, 'If we turn the iPhone into a platform, outside developers will bring hundreds of thousands of applications to the table.' Previous smartphone development platforms looked like government does now: vendors talking in a back room and deciding what features to offer. But then Apple turned the iPhone into a platform in which the killer feature was that other people can make features."

O'Reilly believes that investing in a Web platform—opening data, creating open APIs so anyone can build useful apps—is simply a continuation of the government's historical investment in other platforms. "The highway system was a platform investment," he said. "The post office was another."

Roger Ehrenberg notes that investing in government as platform will be costly, as we have to get the legacy architecture cleaned up and then create an environment in which data can be accessed broadly. "But we can't afford not to do it," he told me. "Because even for things like public-works infrastructure projects, the number of people that are needed to maintain cities in this unbelievably inefficient way . . . is too high." Making the big initial investments needed to overhaul our broken systems will save money in the long run and help us remain relevant down the road. "It's a huge task," he concluded, "but that's reinventing government."

Fixing the disastrous state of its current tech systems is government's greatest challenge. Unfortunately, government is hamstrung by

the legacy issue—the fact that many of its existing systems are inefficient and outdated. It's far easier to build from scratch than to start by
trying to modify existing systems.

When I became mayor, the San Francisco Police Department used
something called the CABLE System for crime reporting. It was—
and still is—a relic of a previous age that almost no one knows how
to use anymore, a patchwork, an embarrassment. In seven years as
mayor, I was able to start but never complete a basic communications
upgrade of this system due to competing public-safety priorities.

Here's another consequence of legacy systems: In September 2011,
when the rankings for countries with the fastest Internet downloads
came out, where was the United States? Not in the top ten. Not even in
the top twenty. We were ranked number twenty-six. The top five countries were South Korea, Romania, Bulgaria, Lithuania, and Latvia—
all countries that were able to build their systems from scratch, without
the legacy burden.

It's almost a joke—South Koreans can get fast broadband connection pretty much anywhere they go. But in Silicon Valley, the epicenter
of the Internet revolution, we drive around dropping cell phone calls
left and right and desperately search for a Starbucks if we need to get
online. This is ridiculous. And it's unsustainable. By letting ourselves
fall so far behind the rest of the wired world, we compromise our productivity and creativity. We can't compete.

"You need a fundamental transformation," says O'Reilly. "You
can't just keep iterating on the old version. . . . New economies in other
parts of the world are going to bypass us unless we really have that
courage [to transform]."

O'Reilly points to the courage of Steve Jobs as the model to follow,
however difficult that may be. "He was fairly unique in having that
kind of leadership, of actually being willing to throw away the old and

start fresh," said O'Reilly. He cites three ways government can do that: (1) recognizing the need for fundamental transformation, (2) establishing simple rules that are market enablers, and (3) focusing on the strategic changes that can allow society to solve its own problems. Doing those three things, he says, will lead to the most important outcome of all: "We have to get away from the vending machine analogy," he says. No more shaking the machine when we don't get what we want; open APIs and government as a platform will allow people to bypass the vending machine altogether.

## THE BLUE BUTTON

In 2010, the nonprofit Markle Foundation wanted to make it easier for US military veterans to access their health data. At the time, there was no simple way for vets to get their various medical records. In fact, the number-one FOIA request to centers for Medicare and Medicaid Services was for health information. This was a frustrating and unnecessary burden for vets to bear.

So Markle decided to develop something called the Blue Button. Here's how it would work: A veteran looks at the Veterans Administration Web site. There's a big blue button on the screen. The vet clicks on it. His or her medical records immediately download in readable, savable form.

And that's it. That's the whole idea in a nutshell. Markle announced the project on August 31, 2010, and on October 7—less than six weeks later—they announced that the Blue Button was up and running. For the first time, vets could download their personal health information in one easy step. Todd Park, the CTO of the United States (formerly of the Health and Human Services Department), told me, "We didn't think it was such a big deal at the time. . . . Privately, when the VA was thinking about success for the Blue Button, they thought maybe twenty-five thousand vets would download."

In fact, some people wondered whether the VA was going too far. "We got inquiries from the private sector," said Park. "People were asking if, under HIPAA [the Health Insurance Portability and Accountability Act], it was legal for people to get their own info." Park assured them it was. "The Blue Button is based on the premise that it's not *our* data, it's *your* data, and you should be entitled to a copy of it." Park was right on the money—that's exactly the open-data stance a government official should take.

Word spread quickly about the Blue Button, and when I met with Park in the summer of 2011—less than a year after its launch—nearly a half million veterans, members of the military, and Medicare beneficiaries (the Department of Defense and Medicare had also implemented the Blue Button) had downloaded their own health information. It was a number beyond anyone's wildest imagining. Yet that was only the beginning. "Others started blue-buttoning their data, too," Park told me. "Aetna, United Health, Walgreens, . . . and the Robert Wood Johnson Foundation launched BlueButtonData.org, where you can learn how to deploy your own Blue Button and publicly commit to doing it."

The VA's Blue Button became a springboard, with others jumping in when they saw how successful it was. And this was the case not only with new Blue Buttons, but also with new apps that worked with Blue Buttons. As Park told me, "We learned that publishing the data was only five percent of the work. Ninety-five percent was making sure that innovators knew it existed and was available. We simultaneously engaged in iterating, growing the campaign to publicize the availability of the data."

The result? "We partnered with Health 2.0, government agencies, foundations," he said. "Companies posted their own challenges to build the best data-powered app. They put on data-related challenges." So the Blue Button—as useful and valuable as it is on its own—became something even bigger. It became a platform.

And that, as Eric Ries, the author of *The Lean Startup*, told me, "jump-starts a new marketplace. Nobody has a great idea the first time out of the gate. Nobody, ever. You have to iterate and change and pivot," Ries said when I interviewed him in San Francisco. "The challenge is to have a framework where you can think big. If you think about the Blue Button, one interpretation is literally that it is *a* button on *a* web page with some data behind it. Like, whoop-de-do. . . . What have you really accomplished at that point?" But the point is, he said, "They're thinking big. It's 'start small, think big.' They're thinking big about the change you *could* catalyze once you get this thing going. Getting the Blue Button on the page was step one of a very complicated multistep process that maybe one day will lead to us having a national electronic health records system. . . . I think that approach is much more likely to succeed than having Congress mandate national health records."

That is the true success of the Blue Button. It's a combination, as Ries says, of big vision and an ability to scale and grow. "When government tries to become innovative, 'that's just code for more giveaways to these contractors.' There's a deep, deep cynicism about it. . . . Anything that breaks that narrative is really important."

Once the Blue Button became an obvious success, it spawned other button ideas. In September 2011, then White House CTO Aneesh Chopra challenged energy companies to create a Green Button, allowing consumers to download all the data on their energy usage. Less than a year later, in January 2012, two companies—PG&E and San Diego Gas & Electric—put Green Buttons on their Web sites.

By the time the Green Button came around, it was clear that the real value went beyond data itself. True, being able to download your own data would encourage consumers to monitor and cut back on their energy consumption. But the real value would come when entrepreneurs and programmers created other applications for that data. Ted Reguly, San Diego Gas & Electric's director of customer programs and assistance, nailed it when he said, "With customers in charge of how the information is used, we anticipate the data will be used in ways we haven't even thought of yet." Or as Todd Park put it, "Raw Green-Button data isn't supercompelling to consumers. But in the hands of developers, it can turn into magic."

Matylda Czarnecka explained in a February 2012 *TechCrunch* blog post what all this could mean in terms of energy costs:

> The interesting aspect isn't so much the download itself, but what can be done with it. Federal officials hope this kind of data liberation will inspire developers to build apps and services that will help customers track and reduce their energy consumption. One study showed that subjects who were given access to their data reduced their usage by 8.7 percent just by tracking it. At scale, this could mean an annual savings of $32 billion per year on the country's annual $369 billion power bill.

The Blue Button and Green Button were the first in a whole rainbow of buttons on the way. Next up was the Department of Education's Purple Button, allowing people to download education information. Anywhere there's useful government data, there should be a button for people to access it. It really is that simple.

## KEEP IT SIMPLE, STUPID

I've always loved the acronym KISS—for "keep it simple, stupid." Too often, we wildly overstate things as being complex when they're not. My staff hates it when I say this, but I truly believe that governing is easier than we like to think it is; it's usually the politicians who over-complicate everything, and that's why people get so disconnected.

Many of the things I'm arguing in this book can be boiled down to this: We've got to simplify, pull back all these layers of supposed complexity, and get down to the essentials. If we want people to engage with government, we should use the same tools that are getting them engaged with companies and institutions in private life. If we want people to care about public issues, we should give them a way to understand and get involved in them. I truly believe that it's not the problems we face that are complex—it's the system we've designed to solve them that's complex. Yet we hold on to that system because it's the way we've always done things.

Not long ago, I looked at the business plan for the first year of my PlumpJack wine store. It was hilarious—if we followed anything remotely like it now, the store would go out of business, and I'd have succeeded only in failing. Everyone knows you can't run a business on the same plan year after year. Yet that's what we've always done in government: "Well, that's what the plan says!" And if someone deviates from it, if someone dares to stick out like the proverbial nail, he or she is hammered down. There's no flexibility, no ability to adapt.

Little by little, that is changing. Aneesh Chopra told me, "There are two Washingtons. There are data-driven, thoughtful problem solvers, and there are people who fall prey to politicization." Todd Park is a great example of the former—a person who came from an entrepreneurial background, bringing that crucial problem-solving skill set to government service.

Alec Ross is another. A senior adviser for innovation to Secretary of State Hillary Clinton, Ross taught with Teach For America before cofounding One Economy, a nonprofit aimed at closing the digital divide. After working for Barack Obama's campaign in 2008, he joined the State Department in April 2009.

Ross is one of a new breed of tech-driven thinkers—a civil servant who isn't bound by the tradition and rigidity so rife in government service. He's focused on how to use the tools of new technology—primarily mobile phones and social networks—to further US diplomacy. Secretary Clinton, for her part, is so fully behind Ross's efforts that he has called her the "godmother of twenty-first-century statecraft."

In early 2010, the whole world got to see the benefits of this new tech-minded approach. On January 12 of that year, a magnitude 7.0 earthquake destroyed much of Haiti, killing hundreds of thousands and rendering a million others homeless. The country was in desperate need of food, water, medical supplies, and other humanitarian aid. And timing was critical—with every day that went by, more people's lives were in danger.

Ross and others at the State Department met to figure out a simple, fast, reliable way to get aid to Haiti. Very quickly, they hit on an idea: How about letting people use their mobile phones to send a donation? If people could just text the word *Haiti* to a dedicated number, they wouldn't have to worry about e-mails, phone calls, Web site URLs, or even credit-card numbers. They'd send that one-word text, and the charge would just appear on their next cell-phone bill. . . . What could be easier than that?

Fortunately, Ross had set up a dinner just the previous week for Secretary Clinton to meet a variety of tech leaders. One of those, James Eberhard, was the CEO of Mobile Accord—a mobile-platform company that could set up mobile donations through its mGive arm. After a few phone calls, the team was able to set up easy text donations to the American Red Cross through all major cell-phone carriers. And within hours after the earthquake, the Text Haiti campaign was up and running.

Ross wasn't sure how much the Text Haiti campaign would raise. He hoped for maybe a couple hundred thousand dollars, maybe more. Every little bit would help. To his astonishment, 2 million Americans texted for Haiti within the first five days, raising more than $22 million. People were texting their friends and family, urging them to donate. They were posting on Facebook and Twitter, commenting on blogs, spreading the number—90999—far and wide. The twin powers of social networking and mobile phones were harnessed to amazing effect, and within three weeks, Text Haiti had raised more than $30 million. "This is a tipping point," mGive's Brad Blanken told a reporter. And it all came about because someone in government was willing to try something new—a simple, tech-based solution to a most basic humanitarian need.

There's another fantastic outcome of all this, in that all the many players feel engaged in the solution. They own it. When Alec Ross convenes a dinner with tech CEOs, then calls on them to assist in a time of crisis, they naturally feel an elemental pull toward helping. The government doesn't have to take everything on itself; it can and should enlist the help of people who are able to help. And including them in the process makes them even more eager to help.

Aneesh Chopra said much the same thing about the Green Button.

"The federal government isn't paying for this," he said. "It can't necessarily require it. But the government plays the role of impatient convener: We met with the CEOs of the energy companies, and they agreed to do this. In one day.

"Those things don't require procurement," he went on. "And they scale naturally"—a crucial element if a project or initiative is to survive. "It's returning to an earlier notion of *commonwealth;* the more futuristic these tools are, the more they're bringing us back to an earlier time." And now that Chopra put the *p* word out there, let's be honest: breaking the cycle of procurement is one of the biggest reasons we must move to government as platform.

## BREAKING THE OLD BOYS' NETWORK

The amount of money government spends to buy things—from professional services to goods—is staggering. The amount of money spent on cars, paper, or consultants is out of control. The very word *procurement* is enough to send chills up the spine of anyone who cares about how government does business.

Procurement—the government's process of purchasing goods or services from third parties—is expensive, time consuming, and often corrupt. It's often about taking care of those who've always done business with the buyer, and it's very hard for new bidders to get any kind of contract. Procurement is like an old boys' network, a process that has little to do with efficiency and everything to do with backslapping and networking.

In the meritocratic world of apps, anyone can create one, and anyone can make money. As long as your app does what it's supposed to do, which is draw people into downloading and using it, you will succeed. There are no secret handshakes, no backroom deals. Good work is rewarded.

Tim O'Reilly asked, "What if there were a market for government services, or governmentlike services, where people could say, 'Oh, I can actually meet that need!' and there was a government apps store that wasn't 'Here are a bunch of apps the government developed' but 'Hey, we're gonna let you figure out how to compete with the government'?" Government doesn't have to create everything; it just has to let others create.

Of course there would have to be rules, just as Apple has its rules for creating apps. "Let's make private services peers with public," O'Reilly says. The more data the government opens up, the more we can create. For example: The Microsoft Bing search engine uses Health and Human Services data to create much more useful searches for hospitals. Google Transit uses government transportation data to provide people more complete information about traveling. The possibilities are literally endless.

"I had a conversation with Mark Zuckerberg about social geography in cities," O'Reilly went on. "The city of San Francisco may have a Facebook presence. But if you wanted to have a really interesting Facebook presence, you'd be able to do something citizencentric. Cities could work with Facebook on how do we issue data so you could say, 'Here's my address,' and it would tell you, 'Here's your trash collection schedule, here's your local police precinct'? Because all these things have different geographies. But it could be done where you provide your address and get back your own social network with the city. It's all there," O'Reilly concludes. "The system just needs to be turned on its head."

## THE DIGITAL CITY

That's exactly what New York City mayor Michael Bloomberg did in 2011, when he appointed twenty-seven-year-old Rachel Sterne as the city's first chief digital officer. Sterne, who had never worked in government, had no public-policy experience, and had managed only a small staff at her start-up, GroundReport, wasn't the most obvious hire to head a major new initiative in a city the size of New York, but she had what we need more of in government: a tech background, an open mind, and a fearless nature.

Sterne spent her first ninety days in office trying to "assess the state of the digital city," as she put it. She and her team analyzed the thousands of ways New Yorkers connect with their government, through NYC.gov, social media, mobile applications, and any other public-facing technology, in an effort to find out what worked and what needed work. The result was a sixty-eight-page report titled *Road Map for the Digital City*—a blueprint for how to propel New York into the digital age.

I sat down with Sterne six months into her tenure to ask how things were unfolding so far. "As part of the *Road Map*, we did an enormous amount of feedback gathering from the public and from agencies," she told me. "And the first thing you realize is, there are hundreds of people across the city who have been trying for years to do the same ten things that you are proposing. And there are reasons that have stopped them from happening. So the will is there, the innovative spirit is there. But the aligning of the stars to make it [happen] isn't always there."

Sterne knew she needed to find a way to harness all that creative energy. She needed to provide platforms where private citizens and entities were free to create new apps, tools, mash-ups—anything that might help the city. "We got a lot of input from the agencies," she told me. "We met with all the social-media managers . . . we met with them and said, 'What do you need to do your job better? What kind of support would help you?'" She also invited the private sector to join in, publicizing her Twitter and Facebook pages so people could communicate with her directly whenever they wanted to.

By opening up city government, Sterne was able to create an environment where innovation was welcomed and rewarded. New York held its first hackathon in July 2011, when more than a hundred developers, designers, and others spent two days working collaboratively to redesign the city's official Web site, NYC.gov. The city also created an open-data API platform and an "apps hub" to showcase new apps. Like Todd Park and Alec Ross, Sterne wanted to do more, open more, create more. "Our challenge," she told a reporter, "is how can we put even more power into the hands of citizens? How can we give them the resources to solve their own problems and meet their own needs?"

By the end of Sterne's first year, New York City had more than 200 social-media channels with more than 1.5 million followers. Successful initiatives ranged from a Bike Share crowdsourcing map to a healthy-recipe tumblr (a microblogging and social-sharing site), and the city also launched its first official Twitter account at @NYCGov. And there was more on the way: an online "dashboard" where residents could see at a glance all of their interactions with the city, from parking tickets to 311 requests to the status of permits. "We have all that data," Sterne told me. "It's just in eight different systems." Creating a one-stop spot for residents to interact with the city "may seem obvious in the private sector," Sterne said, but it's a new concept for government.

All these initiatives are not only new, they're cool. That's the dirty little secret about opening up city data for apps: People don't create boring things; they create really fun, exciting things—like the mash-up of Yelp restaurant listings with the city's Health Department rat-ings. Wouldn't you like to know, when you're planning a dinner out, whether the restaurant you're making a reservation for is rated A, B, or C by the Health Department? Soon you'll be able to do this. Your phone will even send you a warning if you're approaching a restaurant with a poor rating.

The idea is to make possible any combination of cool new tech-nology plus city information. This is how New York ended up with #askmike—a Twitter hashtag that sends your question, comment, or complaint directly to the mayor, who responds to these tweets by post-ing video answers on YouTube. New York also followed San Francis-co's lead in creating a 311 for Twitter, so residents can upload pictures of potholes to goad the city into action. No more waiting on hold for a 311 operator.

The list goes on: You can scan a QR code—those now ubiquitous black squares with unique embedded codes—posted at a construction site to find out how long it'll be before the sidewalk opens back up. You can check a citywide tumblr for information on what's happening in digital NYC on any given day. And recently the city released its data on wheelchair accessibility to pave the way for apps showing people which public restrooms, parks, and buildings are accessible. "The open-data apps are great," Sterne told me. "We didn't spend resources on those, and it's a great value, and it improves people's lives."

Sterne has also learned a few things along the way. "Citizens aren't interested in seeing the world divided by agency," she said. "They want it divided by interest." So instead of having all information about health contained on one giant Health Department page, the city instead puts up separate pages for each topic. For example, the city created a Facebook page called "NYC Quits Smoking." People share tips on quitting, success stories, frustrations, and encouragement. "It doesn't feel city owned," Sterne told me. "It's a public forum that the city happens to be taking care of, keeping clean."

Similarly, the city launched an iPhone app called NYC Condom Finder—one of its biggest initiatives. The app uses GPS and city data to alert users to the five closest places where they can get free condoms. "Initially the kinds of questions they were asking people gave some concern to our communications folks," said Sterne. "But then they quickly realized, this is how to create a real, meaningful dialogue that people participate in."

That is the most crucial element of all these apps. "Ultimately, it doesn't matter if we're not improving people's lives," said Sterne. "That's what this should do. It should be an extension of all government services, exchanging information by embracing all these new platforms. It's relevant to your life, because it's now happening the way you live your life—on your terms. . . . We want to make things easier, faster, so you feel a deeper relationship to your city government."

But here's what's really interesting about all this: It's often not clear right away what will be useful or what kind of apps will improve our lives. Remember Eric Ries's observation: "Nobody has a great idea the first time out of the gate. . . . You have to iterate and change and pivot." We must be open not only to new apps, but also to the evolution of those apps. Something that seemed like a merely OK idea at the time might well evolve into something that changes the world.

"The trajectory of Twitter, to me, really started with Blogger," Twitter cofounder Evan Williams says. "I created Blogger in 1999 for a very personal thing—'Hey, I'll write a script that will make it easier to post a thought to my Web site.' I wasn't really thinking of democratization of publishing. But once we released the product, that's what we realized it was about."

Blogs, says Williams, were a tool that made it practical for anyone to write and express an opinion. "They were considered trivial for the first few years, much like Twitter" he told me. "But then came 9/11, after which a lot of the political bloggers started. Then every campaign had a blog." Yet when Williams took a job at Google in 2003, "even Google didn't have a blog. They sent e-mails to reporters to get the word out about stuff."

Over the next five years, blogging exploded. "For many years," Williams told me, "I thought about what it would mean once everyone had a way to publish their thoughts and voice their opinions. I was seeing it globally, too—I was getting letters from women in Iran who could never write or tell these stories anywhere before. Then later, bloggers were being arrested. . . ." That was when Williams knew this technology was transformational. "Twitter was a continuation of that," he said. "It was, 'Let's lower the barrier even more. Let's really bring it to everybody, and let's put it on the phone, make it accessible through even the weakest channels, all over the world—even where the only source of information they have may be a dumb phone.'"

Yet Williams could never have foreseen what Twitter would ultimately become. Even the 140-character limit was a relic of the fact that Twitter was at first a text-messaging phenomenon. "We were really focused on SMS [text messaging] at first," said Williams. "A hundred sixty characters minus the length of your username, minus two for the colon and a space. So people could actually send longer messages if they had a shorter username."

At first, Twitter was a social thing. People told each other where they were, what they were eating, what they were thinking. Then in early 2007, as wildfires swept through Southern California, people started tweeting more important information—updates on where the fires were moving and which neighborhoods were being evacuated.

The Los Angeles Fire Department started sending out alerts via Twitter too. "It became *the* source of information; that was the fastest way to disseminate information," said Williams.

Over the next few years, Twitter continued to grow—and to change. But instead of Twitter executives trying to guess how the service should change, they simply gave users the ability to make changes themselves. Instead of trying to predict the future, Twitter let its users create the future. "Users invented the retweet," Williams told me. At first, when users started quoting other twitterers, they would cut and paste the quote into their own feed. The Twitter team realized this wasn't ideal, as people could make changes to the quote, and the reply went to the retweeter rather than the original tweeter. So the Twitter team stepped in and created the "native" tweet, which allows users to essentially forward someone else's tweet, automatically including the person's Twitter handle and photo. "In some ways, it was just a user-interface technical decision," Williams told me. "But it was based on this belief that what it should be about is spreading the most relevant information as rapidly as possible. Twitter's had this strange combination of attributes: It's both very simple and very limited, but in a way that let people do whatever they wanted with it. . . . It's a very simple system that, hopefully, in most cases, stays out of the way."

A blue button that downloads your entire medical history. A one-word text to commit money to Haiti. A dashboard that shows you all your interactions with your city. All these are simple solutions, made possible by simple sets of rules for innovating. As Tim O'Reilly says, "The Internet and the World Wide Web had a few simple rules. And people innovate when you have those kinds of simple systems. When you have heavily overspecified systems, you're actually empowering incumbents who are trying to nail things down and keep them exactly the way they are."

# SIX

# Angry Birds for Democracy

MANOR, TEXAS, is a dusty little prairie town just east of Austin with a population of about five thousand people. Like many small towns, it has a farmers' market, ball fields, a post office, and a downtown park that serves as a gathering place for community events. But unlike most small towns, Manor's park has free wi-fi access. It also has signs adorned with QR (quick response) codes, allowing people with smartphones to find anything from historical facts to construction notices, all of which can be updated on the Web in real time. In fact, the City of Manor was reportedly the first government agency in the United States ever to use QR codes in this way.

And that's not even the coolest tech innovation this little town has pioneered. In 2009, the city launched something called Manor Labs—a platform to encourage people to suggest fixes for city problems. In exchange for participating, people received payment in a made-up currency called innobucks. If you submitted an idea, you got a thousand innobucks. If the city actually implemented your idea, you got a hundred thousand innobucks. You could keep track online of how many innobucks you or your neighbors or the lady down the street were collecting.

Why would anyone care about collecting fake money? The City of Manor came up with real rewards you could buy with your innobucks.

For varying amounts, you could buy a police ride-along or even be mayor for the day. Local businesses and restaurants also got in on the fun, offering coupons for discounts or free appetizers in exchange for innobucks. It's not fake currency—it's civic currency.

Once Manor launched innobucks, people got very excited about racking them up. They started suggesting ideas left and right, participating in government as though it were the most fun thing they'd ever done. When people went away on vacation, they'd immediately interact with city government upon returning, trying to make up for lost time and build up their innobucks stashes. Occasionally, when activity slowed down, the city doubled the amount of innobucks offered—and the floodgate of ideas opened again.

Over time, Manor began implementing some of the better suggestions, such as instituting recurring payments for citizens' utility bills and starting an RSS feed—a real-time, constantly updating feed of information—for public work orders, so people could easily see what the city was up to.

The mastermind behind all this activity was a baby-faced twenty-two-year-old named Dustin Haisler. Although Haisler got his first taste of politics as a campaign volunteer at age eleven, he never planned to make a living in government. He decided to study banking, and as a teenager he did some banking work for Manor. But while still in college, Haisler realized he could do more good by helping the city use technology to solve its budget problems, so he took the position of Manor's chief information officer in 2009.

As Haisler put it, "Manor was really inefficient. It needed new ways of doing things, but we had these budget constraints, so the only option was to finance technology to create those new ways of doing things." It was the age-old problem: You have to spend money to save money.

Yet by taking advantage of technology, Haisler knew he could spend a lot less money to greater effect.

"One problem I saw was the way citizens interacted with the government," Haisler said. "[In the private sector], customer service is incredibly important. But that mentality wasn't there when I got to Manor. So I wanted to flip that. I wanted to make it an enjoyable experience and a fun experience. "We started doing crazy, disruptive projects, like putting QR codes on city signs. Then we started looking at 'How do we engage people in the democratic process? How do we reinvent government?'"

At an age when most people would be happy just to land an entry-level job in city government, Haisler wanted to blow the whole thing up. He initiated a partnership with the Persuasive Technology Lab at Stanford, in hopes of figuring out new ways to increase citizen engagement. "We looked at it as, government agencies are good at getting participation in one-time events," he said. "You can launch a campaign, and people will participate—like National Night Out, or these Neighborhood Watch programs. And they'll come out one time—they'll engage at that one period of time. But people engage once, and then they don't come back. So the question we wanted to answer was, 'How do we get them to want to stay put? How do we get them to stay involved in the process long-term?'"

So Haisler started exploring what the private sector was doing. How did companies engage their customers? How did they engage their employees? Were there any new programs that allowed good ideas to bubble up from below? After doing a little research, Haisler found what he was looking for: Spigit, a company that uses games to help companies increase employee engagement.

At the time, said Haisler, "Game mechanics were still kind of laughed at. People thought of it as gimmicky and not important. But the thing that struck me about game mechanics and the way Spigit was using it was that it made a really complex process of innovation into something that wasn't as intimidating." Could games really be the answer to serious government problems? And would that even be appropriate? Haisler thought he knew the answer.

## A NEW WAVE OF CREATIVITY

Before innobucks, there was no clear path for the people of Manor to make suggestions about how to improve their city. Speak up at a town hall? Start a petition? Send an e-mail? Make a phone call? Send a fax—or even an old-fashioned letter? Any of these efforts could easily fall through the cracks. Without a transparent process, no one would have any idea where a suggestion had gone or whether it was ever taken seriously.

"Think of a traditional suggestion box," said Haisler. "Someone puts in an idea or concept, and it may be revolutionary, but they never know what happens to it. When people put a suggestion in, they never know what happens unless they see it implemented." And the less people knew about the process, the less likely they were to want to take part.

Haisler launched an education campaign so people would understand how Manor Labs would work. "We ran the leader board on our site, and in the newspaper every so often, so even people who weren't online could see what the top ideas were and who the top users were. It definitely took some education. It was one of these things where people didn't really understand why we were doing this. And then when they started to see things getting implemented and ideas becoming solutions, it kind of shifted things. It became less, 'Oh, this is just another take on the suggestion box' and more 'Hey, the city's really wanting us to come up with new ways of doing things.'"

The innobucks system kept track of ideas and feedback online so everyone could see what everyone else was suggesting. And Haisler made sure to put both positive and negative feedback loops on the site so there was no mystery about why some initiatives were picked up and others weren't.

At first, he wasn't sure whether people would like getting negative feedback. But what he found surprised him. Instead of getting angry or giving up, people would go right back to the drawing board to try to fix what wasn't working. As it turned out, people weren't just sending in suggestions to fill up their innobucks accounts. They really wanted to make their ideas work. Innobucks had opened up the system to ordinary people and even made it fun for them to participate. It seemed to be unleashing a whole new wave of creativity.

Haisler understood that that wasn't actually the case, however. "What I realized was that our citizens and governments innovate all the time. There's a lot of noise that's out there on Facebook, on Twitter, and on a lot of other sites; it's just very difficult for government agencies to act on the information." It was impossible for city officials to keep track of which ideas might be worth pursuing, much less come to a consensus on them.

"That's what we sought to use Spigit for—not just to collect feedback, but to allow the crowd, the citizens themselves, to help us decide what we should act upon," said Haisler. "It kind of changed the model of how things have been done, because normally you collect feedback and then hand-pick a few things you want to implement. And you say, 'Yay, we're working together, we're making the whole thing transparent and collaborative.'

"But we actually wanted to make the entire process transparent and allow the citizens to drive it. It's pushing the 'wisdom of the crowds' theory to an extreme," he said. "What I realized in the process was that our citizens were very in tune with what we should do. They were experiencing the problems every day, and it was harder from a top level, from the administration of the city, to identify the problems through the lens of a citizen. So why not just ask them? So we engaged lots of them in conversation, and a lot of really interesting solutions came out of that."

Not only did the City of Manor get some valuable new ideas, but people also managed to have some fun along the way. How often can you say that about a government program?

## ANGRY BIRDS FOR DEMOCRACY

In December 2009, a flock of birds was released upon the world. But not just any birds—Angry Birds.

This unassuming little game, created by a four-person team in Finland for about $140,000, became an instant sensation. It was downloaded more than 50 million times in 2010. It has spent more time as Apple's top paid app than any other game or app. As I write this, Angry Birds has been downloaded more than a billion times across all different platforms, and at any given moment of any day, literally millions of people all over the world are staring at screens, shooting little birds from slingshots at green pigs.

Why do people play Angry Birds? It's easy, it's fun, and it's right there in the palm of your hand. Like Manor's innobucks program, it gets your competitive juices flowing, and you can satisfy your competitive urge anytime you want. Innobucks is like Angry Birds, but for democracy. It's playing and engaging not just for the sake of fun, but for a higher purpose.

There are people who think it's heresy to suggest games as a way of engaging people in government. After all, government is serious business! It's for adults, not kids! If you have to trick people into engaging, goes this line of thinking, they're probably not worth engaging to begin with.

To that I say, baloney. Why not make it fun? Why not do everything we can to draw people in? If certain people—most people, if we're being honest—don't find government engaging, interesting, or worthwhile, why should we assume that's *their* fault? Isn't it possible that it's the *government's* fault?

Tech journalist Greg Ferenstein gets a little worked up when he talks about this. "Voting for president used to be a carnival," he told me. He pointed out that Americans used to get really excited about politics—so much so that in 1776, half a million people bought copies of Thomas Paine's pamphlet *Common Sense*. To give you some perspective, there were only 2.5 million people in the entire United States at the time, so as a percentage of population, more people read *Common Sense* in 1776 than watched the Super Bowl this year. "We used to be a country that thrived on and loved politics," he said. But with the rise of money-fueled, ideological campaigns, the decline of civility, and the complete failure of our government institutions to keep up with technological, social, and generational changes, politics sure isn't fun anymore. So how can we bring back the fun?

"It needs to be targeted toward a large population, and in a varied way that attracts people's interests," Ferenstein told me. "And those platforms are Facebook, to some extent Google, Twitter. . . . It's possible to create platforms where people get involved and do debates. But it just needs to be targeted toward them."

Instead of moving toward targeted engagement, however, we seem to be moving further away from it. Remember the Filter Bubble? Facebook gradually edits out the updates of people who disagree with you politically. So instead of increasing our engagement with each other, we're being artificially kept apart.

"To me, there should be a Facebook application where people can track the things they care about and talk about it with people who disagree with them," says Ferenstein. "If I find out that one of my good friends is a Republican and thinks differently, I want to debate that person. And I want my friends to see that debate. That's what the carnival atmosphere of politics used to be. It used to be fun. And Facebook can do that." The trick is to make politics feel less like work and more like the fascinating, relevant, life-changing exercise that it can truly be. It's feeding people vegetables disguised as cookies.

"We all want to be mayor for a day," says Dustin Haisler. "We want to earn a badge. . . . It's really interesting to see how these fun dynamics can apply to such bureaucratic and boring processes, like master planning. You can turn these things into a game, which helps not only individuals who want to plug in; it also helps the agencies, because they get clear feedback above and beyond the group of people that will regularly show up to a planning and zoning meeting and voice their opinion. . . . It provides a better way for individuals to plug in who may not have the time to go to a meeting."

## SUPERBETTER

Not everyone believes that games are the answer. There are plenty of critics of the "gamification" of serious subjects, and they seem to have found their lightning rod in Jane McGonigal, creator of the online game SuperBetter and author of *Reality Is Broken: Why Games Make Us Better and How They Can Change the World.*

McGonigal came up with the idea of SuperBetter after injuring herself in a freak accident. She hit her head on a cabinet in her office, and the concussion she suffered caused her headaches, vertigo, and nausea for months. At the lowest point of her misery, she felt suicidal, so she asked friends and family to start giving her "missions"—simple tasks she could complete and feel good about. McGonigal then turned that idea into a gaming Web site, raising $1 million to launch what she called "an online, social game designed to help you build up personal resilience."

SuperBetter uses game mechanics to help people achieve serious goals—losing weight, quitting smoking, leaving a bad relationship. Your home page for the game is called your Secret Headquarters, you have a Secret Lab where you can track your progress, and the people who give you missions are called your allies. Critics of McGonigal have lambasted her for using frivolous means to serious ends. In a review of *Reality Is Broken* in the *Wall Street Journal*, Andrew Klavan wrote, "Ms. McGonigal's notions about how to enliven what gamers call 'RL' ('real life') run the gamut from shallow to, well, that's it."

It's easy to criticize efforts like McGonigal's. With all the problems afflicting America today—budget deficits, partisan poison, political gridlock—how can we take seriously the suggestion that games are the answer? Here's how: We have to meet the people where they are. And where they are right now is playing games and spending time on social-networking sites.

A recent Kaiser Family Foundation study showed that American kids between the ages of eight and eighteen spend *fifty-three hours a week* on entertainment media—more hours than a parent typically works in a week. And the true number is even higher, because kids typically multitask, playing games while texting while watching videos on YouTube. So the average kid actually packs more than ten hours' worth of entertainment into a seven-hour session. And three quarters of American households spend time playing games online.

Looking at those numbers, we'd be foolish not to pursue a gaming angle to bring people back into governance. It's not a panacea—we don't want gaming to be the only way people engage—but every bit helps. And the truth is, what we're doing now is failing, so we don't have much to lose.

Remember those *Schoolhouse Rock!* clips on Saturday morning television in the seventies? "I'm just a bill. / Yes, I'm only a bill. And I'm sitting here on Capitol Hill. . . ." In three and a half minutes, that clip educated a generation of American kids as to how laws are made. Television had become the way kids spent their leisure time—so why not take the opportunity to educate them through that same medium? It worked then, and it can work now. Let's meet people where they are.

## PUTTING THE "FUN" IN "FUND-RAISING"

In September 2009, actor/activist Edward Norton, Hollywood producer Shauna Robertson, and entrepreneurs Robert and Jeffro Wolfe launched a new way to raise money for nonprofits. They wanted to "put the fun in fund-raising"—to find a new way to get people excited about raising money.

Norton was planning to run the New York City marathon, and he wanted to raise funds for the nonprofit Maasai Wilderness Conservation Trust. But he wanted to do more than just hand his family and friends brochures and ask them to sponsor his run. So he turned to

Twitter and the Web in search of pledges, and he offered gifts and incentives in return. In less than eight weeks, the team raised an astonishing $1.2 million for the Maasai.

This was the seed of Crowdrise, which bills itself "a unique blend of online fundraising, crowdsourcing, social networking, contests, and other nice stuff." Its tagline—"If you don't give back, no one will like you"—tells you everything you need to know about the spirit of whimsy the Crowdrise team brings to serious pursuits.

Like many fund-raising sites, Crowdrise offers gifts for certain donation levels. Anyone giving seventeen dollars toward scholarships for cancer survivors, for example, would receive a bottle of Sexy Hot Tan sunscreen adorned with a photo of Will Ferrell in a Speedo. The fun was in doing a traditional thing—offering donor thank-you gifts—in a nontraditional way. But more interesting was the unusual way Crowdrise managed to draw in people who couldn't afford to donate money themselves.

The team created something called Crowdrise impact points, or CIPs. You can earn CIPs by doing plenty of things other than donating: raising money from others, getting votes from the Crowdrise community, sending in a photo of yourself wearing a Crowdrise T-shirt or holding a flag, or even answering trivia questions sprinkled throughout the Crowdrise Web site. You can still be one of the most influential people on Crowdrise's site even if you are flat broke. CIPs are "civic currency," reputational rather than monetary.

Like Manor's innobucks, CIPs reward people for getting involved. But here's the interesting part: Unlike innobucks, CIPs can't be traded in for actual goods and services (except for Crowdrise's own merchandise, such as hoodies and T-shirts). CIPs have no real-world value. Yet people obsessively collect them because you can earn enough points to be designated Crowdrise Royalty. Anyone who amasses two hundred thousand points is dubbed a Tsar. Three hundred thousand earns you the title of Mime. Five hundred thousand and you're a Baron. If you get up to a million Crowdrise Impact Points, you're given the highest rank—a Sir or a Dame. And that has proved to be incentive enough for thousands of people to work their tails off for Crowdrise.

I asked cofounder Shauna Robertson about Crowdrise, and she told me the CIP system is one of the site's most popular features. "I enjoy working with City Year," she said—an AmeriCorps program in which young people devote a year to public service—"and they're incredible kids. They become amazing leaders. But they don't have necessarily the money to give or even the community to pull money from. But what they do—they're very active on Crowdrise for points," she said. "So they'll have competitions, or they'll auction something off for the most votes. There's a huge voting system on Crowdrise, where people will vote for the best fund-raisers . . . and there are people who really care about these points."

Crowdrise members happily spend time and energy pursuing points that have no cash value. They also eagerly pursue other virtual "rewards"—often with as much vigor as they pursue real rewards. Robertson told me about a contest in which Crowdrise gave away a Puma bike. You improved your chances of winning by increasing the amount of money you raised. Not surprisingly, people eagerly raised as much as possible—who wouldn't want a cool new bike for free, after all?

"Then we'll do a competition to win an invisible shower cap," Robertson said. And to everyone's surprise, people frantically raise just as much money in hopes of winning that completely nonexistent prize. In the end, it really wasn't about the value of the thing people could win. It was about the winning.

"It's incentivizing people to do something," Robertson told me. "Feeling like, if they get involved they have a chance to win something. Even if they probably are not going to win that thing, they'll come back and donate six or seven times just to enter into that drawing more and more. I talk to some people who win these things, and I'll ask, 'Why did you give more than once?' and they'll tell me, 'Well, I would have given a hundred dollars, but because your prize was for ten dollars, I just entered ten times so then I felt like I could be more a part of this contest.' . . . If their intention is to give a hundred dollars to charity, then let them give how they want."

We might find this surprising, but should we? The truth is, people will spend untold hours doing things that seem to have no redeeming value—even things that seem like chores.

Japanese Tamagotchi are the perfect example: little plastic "pets" that you keep in your pocket and have to care for just like real pets. You have to feed them, discipline them, put them to bed, even clean up after them. I have two toddlers, and I can honestly say it's beyond me why anyone would voluntarily mimic the daily routine of taking care of one. But more than 75 million Tamagotchi have been sold to date, and people seem willing and eager to spend precious time caring for them. If people will do that for nothing but entertainment value, doesn't it follow that they'll do things for government—even things that normally aren't all that fun—if there's a game element to them?

This is Crowdrise's theory behind fund-raising—not ordinarily a very fun activity. "We learned that you can raise a lot of money by making it fun," Robertson told me. Hence the Napkin Crest, a special award for sending a photo of a napkin that gets posted on an official Napkin Page. When Crowdrise created the Napkin Crest, thousands of people immediately began sending in photos. And while those photos themselves might not enrich nonprofits, the fact that people are so engaged just builds the excitement around Crowdrise's Web site and its true mission. "If you can harness that silliness . . . you wouldn't believe how much money you can raise," said Robertson.

## SPENDING REAL MONEY ON REAL THINGS

It's surprising enough that people are willing to put in hours of very real work for nothing more than virtual points and the prestige that comes with them. But here's the kicker: Many people are also willing to pay real money for virtual things.

In December 2011, a company called PlaySpan released research showing that nearly one third of people involved in online multiplayer games have spent real money on virtual goods. More than half of those did so at least once a month. They're purchasing things that have value only in their games—virtual currency, maps, armor, weapons. Some are also willing to spend money just to dress their online avatars in designer clothes.

According to the *Economist* magazine, this practice has become so lucrative that some gaming companies are changing their entire business models. One such game is The Lord of the Rings Online:

> When the game was released in 2007, players had to buy the game for $40 and then pay a subscription for each month they played. Last year Turbine, the game's developers, moved to a new charging model in which the game was made available for nothing, but players could spend real-world money on "Turbine Points," a sort of electronic

currency with which to buy items that make the player more power-ful. Turbine says its revenue from the game tripled.

FarmVille—the inspiration for the notion of Citizenville—works on a similar principle. Players can spend real money to buy virtual coins that allow them to buy virtual livestock and farm equipment—and they do so in droves. In fact, although Zynga makes some money from advertising, the vast majority of its revenues comes from selling virtual goods. As NPR reported in November 2011, "Zynga raked in $1 billion this last year, in sales of virtual tractors that plow virtual farms, or avatars that embody gamers' Web personas."

Crowdrise's Robertson takes us to the obvious next step: "FarmVille doesn't have anything to it other than the pride of collecting those points," she said, "so why can't you have a FarmVille for government?"—especially if you're going to spend real money on it.

In FarmVille, when people spend money to take care of their virtual farm, that money goes into the pockets of the game developers. In Citizenville, people would spend money on actual improvements in the player's neighborhood—say, an hour of professional landscaping or fresh paint to cover up graffiti. In both FarmVille and Citizenville, players have the enjoyment of the game. But in Citizenville, instead of taking pride in a virtual world, players would be making a difference in their own neighborhoods. I don't know about you, but I think that as long as it looked and felt like these other games, Citizenville would be a huge hit. It's the perfect mash-up of gaming and real civic engagement, with the bonus of not only virtual rewards, but real physical rewards. "If the power of the crowd is happy to do these little, weird things," said Robertson, "then I don't know why government can't harness that." There is no reason why not.

## COMMUNICATION, NOT CALCULATION

When you drive down the highway, have you ever noticed the occasional signs indicating that a particular stretch has been "adopted" by a group or company? This is a tremendously popular government initiative that started in the mideighties—people were happy to take responsibility for keeping a highway shoulder clean, because they could post a sign letting everyone know they were doing it. Their good citizenship provided them with social capital.

That was the 1.0 version of Citizenville: getting out with plastic bags and picking up garbage in exchange for a road sign you hoped people might notice as they whizzed by on the interstate. The 2.0 version is digital: It has an online scoreboard, social networking, and interactive maps. Citizenville 2.0 takes advantage of new technology in order to better solve age-old problems.

These kinds of digital solutions are more crucial than ever, because the 1.0 world is being phased out, and it's not ever coming back. Nearly half of the US population—about 140 million of our residents—is under the age of thirty. And people under the age of thirty literally grew up with the Internet. They are not *learning* to live digitally. They *are* digital, to the core—digital natives.

Under-thirties are often referred to as millennials, but Don Tapscott has dubbed them the net generation. "The defining characteristic of this generation is not that 2000 came and went," he told me. "This is the net generation: They're the first to come of age in the digital age. They have no fear of technology, just as you have no fear of a refrigerator. They want a different approach, and they have very different views of government. They're prepared to self-organize, to make things happen." They are also tremendously idealistic, but they don't connect that to government. Young people simply don't think of public spirit or public service when they think of government.

Shawn Allen of Stamen Design, the company behind Oakland's Crimespotting tool, says, "I feel divorced from the decision-making process that tends to happen. Overcrowded community meetings, supervisor hearings—it all leaves me feeling disconnected. I read about things after the fact. I feel unable to affect change in anything that doesn't involve my skill set. I would love to see a willingness from the city to engage younger people on the platform where they exist." He's right—if we in government continually try to communicate with people in a language they no longer speak, they won't be interested in hearing what we have to say. FDR effectively used radio when television was in its infancy. But any contemporary politician who relied on radio today would seem like a fossil. And television was king for the second half of the twentieth century—but anyone who thinks he or she can command the country's attention today solely by making television appearances is mistaken.

This is the age of Facebook, Twitter, and YouTube. If you want to appeal to the vast population of young people in this country, you'd better learn how to use these tools to your advantage. Bill Clinton saw this firsthand when the video *Clinton Foundation: Celebrity Division*—a spoof of celebrity activism starring such A-listers as Matt Damon, Kristen Wiig, Sean Penn, Ted Danson, and Mary Steenburgen—drew far more attention than anything he'd ever put online. "I don't have all that many Facebook followers," he told me. "It's not an emotional cutting edge to everything we do. But we had 1.2 million people download that funny video." As Stewart Brand says, "Computers are not calculation devices. They are communication devices." If we in government are to successfully communicate with young people, we must understand that.

# WE ARE ALWAYS ONLINE

Eric Schmidt, the executive chairman of Google, has described American young people as having "two states: asleep or online." And it's true. Just as people today would never describe themselves as "being on the electricity grid," young people don't think of themselves as being online. With smartphones, iPads, and laptops, they're never *not* online. For the vast majority of Americans, there's no such thing as dialing up or going online anymore. It's simply a constant state.

And that's not the only way the net generation is different. For his 2008 book *Grown Up Digital,* Don Tapscott surveyed more than eleven thousand young people in a $4 million research study. He found eight characteristics common to those in the net generation: (1) freedom, (2) customization, (3) scrutiny, (4) integrity, (5) collaboration, (6) entertainment, (7) speed, and (8) innovation.

The Internet has been central in developing all of these traits, but most interesting for the notion of Citizenville are (5) collaboration and (6) entertainment. As Tapscott wrote about collaboration, people in the net generation "discuss brands, companies, products and services," and they "want to work hand-in-hand with companies to create better goods and services." Their relationships are defined by collaboration.

For previous generations, the relationship between customer and business was more formal, more defined. A company might take note of what was or wasn't selling in its stores and shift its inventory accordingly, but the notion of "collaborating" in any sustained way with customers was unheard of. Apart from filling out the occasional customer survey, sending a letter, or just bending the ear of a cashier, there wasn't really any way you could offer feedback to a company.

But now companies get constant real-time feedback via their Web sites, Yelp, Twitter mentions, Facebook pages. . . . Brand-new channels have sprung up through which people can easily have their say—and be heard. And the net generation has never known it any other way, so it expects this to be the case now and forever.

Then, of course, there's (6) entertainment. As Tapscott wrote in his book, "This generation brings a playful mentality to work . . . and has been bred on interactive experiences." People like to be entertained—and for the first time in history, they can be entertained no matter what they're doing or where they are, as long as they have their smartphones with them. And as of mid-2012, more than half of all US cell phone subscribers have smartphones—a tremendous jump from just a year earlier, when only 38 percent had them.

Games used to be something we played at home or in gatherings of friends. Now they're something we play whenever we have a free minute or two in line at the movies or waiting at the doctor's office. With smartphones, playing games is a part of our everyday lives.

This is also the first time in history that people are entertaining themselves with the same tools through which they communicate. Think about it: For generations Americans got their news and information from newspapers, magazines, radio, and television. These were all one-way conduits, where information traveled from news provider to consumer. Now, more and more Americans get their news and information from Internet sources, which they consume through their smartphones. Yet these also happen to be the devices on which they play their games—Words with Friends, Angry Birds, Draw Something.

For a young person, the blend of all these elements—communication, information, and entertainment—is seamless. Games are simply a part of everyday life, and entertainment is something you can find at the touch of a button. It all comes through your smartphone, so it's all part of the same quilt of communication. The bright dividing lines between entertainment and more serious information have disappeared.

So when government wants to capture the attention of young people, as Greg Ferenstein says, "It should be fun . . . it has to be social. And it has to be habitual." Just as they do with FarmVille, for Citizenville we want people to have regular interaction, to feel fully engaged. When people feel engaged, they feel ownership—and that's when they truly start giving their time and energy to something.

## CUTTING-EDGE TECHNOLOGY AND CULTURAL RELEVANCE

Age isn't the only demographic that matters in this shift. Latinos of all ages are on the cutting edge of new technology, and the more we can incorporate social media and texting, the greater their civic participation will be.

Maria Teresa Kumar, the executive director of Voto Latino, explains how crucial it is to pay attention to this growing demographic. "There are 1.2 million Latinos turning eighteen every two years," she told me when I sat down with her at the Clinton Global Initiative meeting in New York City. "That's 1.5 congressional districts. And they're not apathetic—it's just that no one is asking them to vote. We need to get people registered, remind them to vote, give out voter guides."

And the best ways to get people engaged, she says, are through technology. Voto Latino "connects with people on Facebook. We put out the call to meet at events, and people go out and disseminate that information." Voto Latino also uses text messaging to get the information out. "Eighty percent of Latinos are English-dominant," she says.

"We are early adopters in text messaging and social media." Using text messages, she says, led to a huge spike in participation.

"We were able to change the conversation. We're modernizing how we talk to the Latino community. We did a project with iTunes, where if you took the census, you would receive twenty-five songs on iTunes. We were able to get the message out this way—and it was interesting because it was also a great win for iTunes . . . it was also good for the census because people filled it out who otherwise wouldn't have." Win-win.

Voto Latino also engaged Latinos by using celebrities who have cachet in the community. "We have a coalition of thirty-five celebrities," Kumar told me. "They do public-service announcements, voter registration—we put them to work!" For the census project, Voto Latino asked their celebrities to tweet about it and urge people to take part. "There was one woman in the Central Valley who saw a tweet from Demi Lovato," said Kumar. "She took it to her church and got dozens of people to do the census. If you give people tools and a map, they will run with it," she said. "We've been around for a while, but now we're packaging things in a way that's culturally relevant and exciting for people."

## WHY THE MUNI ISN'T FREE

While I was mayor, I learned that charging people to ride SF Muni— San Francisco's municipal trains—wasn't bringing the city any real money. The tickets were just $1.50 each, and the costs of collecting money, buying and maintaining fare boxes, and catching fare cheats rendered negligible whatever profit the city was making. So I told my staff I wanted to make Muni free. Why go to the trouble of collecting fares if they didn't really bring in any money? Why not just eliminate the hassle?

My staff advised against it, for two reasons. One was that if we made riding the trains free, ridership was estimated to increase by 35 to 40 percent. We'd have to add more trains, costing the city money. That made sense, but it was the second reason—a reason I'd never considered—that really gave me pause. If we made traveling on Muni free, went the argument, people would then treat it like a free system. They'd trash it.

Margaret Cliver, a resident of the Mission District, made this point colorfully in an interview with a reporter: "Gavin Newsom must have taken a leave of his senses to even consider this. MUNI is already overloaded with stinky crazies, loud-mouth-behaved louts, and other zoological forms of low life. The day it becomes entirely free, it will become a Dumpster on wheels, and I, along with the rest of those who currently attempt to use the system, will give up on it entirely."

If people have no investment in something, they'll treat it like a throwaway. People need to feel ownership. That is the message that Dustin Haisler, who's now the director of government innovation at Spigit, takes to the government agencies he advises. "One thing that I always tell agencies now is find people who are already vocal in the community, and let them become champions of the site. This isn't something that should be controlled and run by city hall. This should be something that's community powered and community owned," he said. With innobucks, "Having the mentality that this was a *community* platform, we were just catalysts to help the conversation flow." Because people felt the site was theirs, not the government's, they were more eager to participate.

DonorsChoose, Kiva, and Kickstarter are perfect examples of this theory at work. Consider DonorsChoose: Potential donors can go online and choose exactly which project they'd like to give to, and they can see exactly how much it will cost and how much has already been pledged. They are in control of their own giving at every moment, even choosing whether to designate a portion of their donation to covering administrative costs. And once a project has been fully funded, the teacher and students send thank-you notes to the donors, making them feel even more connected.

This a wonderful system, and it funds many worthwhile projects. But to my surprise, DonorsChoose founder Charles Best told me that funding these projects isn't really the point. Yes, he agreed, it's fantastic for teachers to get supplies they can't afford, but Best is after something bigger. "We see the significance of our site not in the dollar value of resources delivered," he told me. "Even at $100 million, we'd be taking a fractional bite out of teacher out-of-pocket spending, let alone system underfunding." Right now, Best said, teachers are spending more than $1 billion a year of their own money, so in real terms, the donations provided by DonorsChoose are just one tenth of what teachers are taking from their own pockets for school supplies.

So what's the point? "It's in the people who would otherwise not be engaged with public schools and who otherwise would not have a window into classrooms in low-income communities and would not feel a personal relationship with a classroom on the other side of the tracks— a relationship which we believe is top-of-mind when they go into the voting booth," he told me. "Sixty percent of our donors say they're more interested in reforming the system after being on our site, because it was their first really vivid encounter with what's going on in public schools." That's the buy-in he's looking for—because that's the kind of buy-in that leads to long-term, deeper involvement with schools and kids.

The same holds true for government projects. When New York

City launched its Bike Share program, it included an interactive online map to which anyone could add a tag to suggest a location for Bike Share racks. NYC chief digital officer Rachel Sterne's team would assess those locations, choosing the best for new racks. "When that happens, you feel like, 'Wow, that's the place I suggested!'" Sterne told me. "You feel ownership."

Why not offer a token reward for whoever has the most bike-rack suggestions implemented? It doesn't have to be anything fancy or expensive—a rubber-ducky bike bell or a camouflage bike-helmet cover will do—anything that will get people talking about the project, sending in suggestions, and telling their friends. Anything that will make people feel like engaging with their government can be fun and competitive. If we can replicate that thrilling feeling of punching in your initials after getting the high score on a video game, we can get people excited about doing real good.

# SEVEN

# The X Factor

ONE AFTERNOON IN THE SUMMER OF 2004, a guy named Jeremy Stoppelman got the flu. Stoppelman, a former VP of engineering at PayPal, had just moved back to the Bay Area after spending a year at Harvard Business School, and he didn't have a regular doctor. So he decided to look for one online.

"I did a search for doctors on Google," he told me. "I ended up on insurance Web sites and basic directory sites. But I really couldn't find anything that said who's actually good, like 'What do people think of this person?'" He could find lists of doctors, with information on where they practiced and where they went to medical school. Yet there was no way to find out what kind of reputation a doctor had. "Here was a real, meaty, unsolved problem," Stoppelman said.

"I thought to myself, *How do we deal with this offline?* The old-world solution was, you ask a bunch of friends for recommendations—word of mouth. So that got me thinking, *Wow, is there a way that we can bring word of mouth to the Web?*" Would it be possible to replicate the experience of getting friends' personal recommendations on a Web site? Stoppelman decided it would be.

"We started the service"—soon dubbed Yelp—"by asking friends for recommendations," he told me. "And one thing that stood out, that really worked, was that some people really wanted to share their recommendations. It wasn't so much that people wanted to ask questions and have a Q and A, which was the original angle. It really became about being a platform for those who had the time and inclination [to share their opinions]." But when people started reviewing, they got most passionate about reviewing restaurants.

It was the perfect way to draw people into Yelping. Everybody has an opinion about restaurants, after all. And once they got into it, people started reviewing all kinds of other things, too—prisons, post offices, departments of motor vehicles, parks, even bus lines. You can review pretty much anything on Yelp, as long as it has an address, is public, and is of popular interest. That includes, as Stoppelman told me, things as esoteric as the fountain of the *Star Wars* character Yoda in San Francisco's Presidio (seventy-six reviews, four and a half stars out of five).

In the eight years since its founding, Yelp has become an indispensible tool for many. More than 60 million people use it every month, searching mostly for reviews of local businesses. And with every user who posts a review, the value of the site grows. People go to Yelp to find a place to eat; they eat at that place; and then they post their own review. The more reviews, the more value the site adds, and the self-sustaining feedback loop goes on. One-way is dead; two-way is the future.

What can we in government learn from this? Businesses make adjustments and improvements all the time based on criticisms in their Yelp reviews. As Stoppelman told me, the reaction of businesses to Yelp's rise has been, "It's really put me on my A game, because anyone who walks through the door can review me."

Is there some way we could harness this kind of feedback loop to improve government services? I asked Stoppelman whether Yelp has delved into politics at all. "You generally can't review people," he told me, but you can review government services. "Most of the reviews on public transport, especially bus lines, is just people venting," he said. San Francisco's Department of Parking and Traffic gets one and a half stars, for example. And the Department of Public Health gets two and a half. Not too impressive—but is anyone listening?

"It could be useful to have someone in the city government who monitors that stuff," says Stoppelman, "but it's mostly like an exhaust valve." Yet Stoppelman has a point—it would be tremendously useful to monitor these reviews, for one big reason. Government entities, unlike restaurants or bars or movie theaters or bowling alleys, have no real competition. If you don't like your city's garbage collection, you can't switch to another one. If your local DMV is terrible, you're stuck. Government is the ultimate monopoly. And monopolies, as any economist will tell you, often breed complacency and a lack of innovation.

Yet what if you *could* create competition among city services—much like the competition among people in Manor, Texas, to collect the most innobucks—through a kind of government Yelp? Then we'd be on to something.

First, you could set up an intracity competition among departments, with a Yelp-style scoreboard showing who has the highest rating. Let's say the health department has two and a half stars, the DMV just two, and the police department four and a half—the police department wins for the month! There could be prizes, or even bonuses, for the departments that earn the most consistent high scores. Why not set up competition with other departments? As we've seen, people will do a lot—and spend a lot and work a lot—to win even virtual prizes online. Why not take advantage of that natural competitiveness?

Second, it's not exactly true that your town's DMV has no competition. It might not have competition within your town—but why not set up a competition with other DMVs in the surrounding areas? In the

New York City area, for example, there could easily be a friendly competition among the DMVs in the five boroughs. Which gives the best service? Which has the highest rating? And more important—how can we get ours higher than those other guys'?

Look at it this way: If the Bronx's DMV comes from behind to overtake Brooklyn for the highest ratings, do you think that will get Brooklyn's competitive juices flowing? I certainly do. It's human nature to compete, and this is the perfect tool for setting up a competition where none existed before. DMV workers from neighboring areas could even have online discussion boards to discuss the competition or to talk about what's working and what's not.

All of this would be incredibly easy and cheap to set up, so whatever improvements it brought would be well worth the relatively small investment. Perhaps then we'd see more comments like the one posted to Yelp by Rosie W. of San Francisco:

> They trimmed all the dangerously dangling dead limbs off the trees on my street. Because I asked them to. They told a city employee that if he wants to continue to drive that city truck, he may not flick his lit cig into a pile of pine needles in front of a grammar school. Because I asked them to. I am drunk with power.

## RATEMYDMV.COM

The reason Yelp is so powerful is that it's user generated. It's not a government-sponsored reviewing committee with a long list of criteria and rules; it's the unvarnished thoughts and feelings of the people who matter most. In business, they're called consumers. In politics, we call them constituents.

Right now, there's no clear feedback loop for government agencies. You can call to complain, or you can send an e-mail or letter, and maybe, if you're lucky, you'll get some kind of response. But like that old-time suggestion box, once the complaint goes in, it's a complete mystery what happens to it afterward. Having a Yelp-style government ratings system will bring transparency to that whole process.

As Stoppelman sees it, this is one of the most effective things about Yelp. "It's not just, 'I'm putting out comment cards, and then I'm getting feedback, and I look at it personally,'" he said. "Yelp puts everyone's laundry out in the open." Businesses have no choice but to react.

Have you ever looked at the Web site RateMyProfessors.com? If you're not in academia, you might not have heard of it. But if you're a professor, you've probably looked at it more times than you'd care to admit. RateMyProfessors.com is a site that allows students to post comments, praise, and complaints about their college professors. Students rate their professors in the categories of helpfulness, clarity, and easiness on a scale of one to five. The site then averages ratings for a professor's "overall quality" score.

Before, in order to find out whether a professor was any good or not, students would have to track down somebody who'd already taken the professor's class. Now the students have much more power. They can share their opinions, offer their ratings, and even track how a professor's reputation has changed over time. This empowers them to make better choices. It also empowers them by creating a public, visible place where professors must face critiques of their work. (Rate MyProfessor.com also lets students rate how good-looking they think their professor is. Like innobucks or invisible shower caps, it's silly and fun—and ultimately useful, as it draws more students and professors to the site.)

So why not create a RateMyDMV.com site? It could be set up the same way as RateMyProfessor.com—with serious categories such as wait time, friendliness, and helpfulness, and then a silly category or two, like quality of coffee, or horribleness of driver's license photos. As people post their ratings, their rants, or their praise, DMV employees can keep track and propose improvements based on the feedback.

It's interesting that China has begun experimenting with this kind of real-time feedback. Vivek Kundra, President Obama's former CIO, told me about going through customs at an airport in China: "They had this simple thing I thought was cool. When I went through customs, there was a sign with a happy face, a sad face, and a flat face. You could point at a picture to rate the agent in real time. The customs agents know that as soon as you're finished, you're rating them!" This is the kind of immediate feedback that businesses and private entities are getting used to and that government should embrace. Once again, one-way is dead, and two-way is the future.

"One big change in today's world is that we're moving to feedback loops in computing that are in real time," Tim O'Reilly told me. "When you use an application like Google Maps, your phone is a sensor reporting to the application where you are right now." Google takes that information and uses it to make refinements in its mapping and directions. The same is true for searches—Google keeps track of which results people click through to, then uses those results to refine future searches. This is the essence of a feedback loop.

"This type of big data and machine learning is what's driving the really interesting applications today. But it's not driving government," O'Reilly said, echoing the common theme: businesses and people are taking advantage of new technologies, but government isn't. "The systems that are starting to work," he told me, "are the ones where there's dynamic feedback interaction in real time."

Stewart Brand used another example to make this point. He told me about Google's AdSense, a system for targeting relevant ads to con-sumers. "They want the ads to be as valuable to you as the organic search results," Brand said. "Ads move up the line based on how happy people are. And advertisers are happy because they're getting the cus-tomers who are actually interested. That kind of virtuous cycle they set in motion here is what we need in government."

Bill Clinton has an idea for getting such a cycle started. "Let's take something really elementary," he said to me. "California still has bud-get problems. . . . So I'm going to give you, every day this week, a problem that I see with reviving broad-based economic prosperity, giving our kids the education they deserve, growing our economy while taking on environmental challenges. And I want you to come back with ideas." In other words, he'd post the problem online and invite people to weigh in.

"Suppose you did that for five or six days in a row, and suppose you never got more than five thousand responses on any day," he went on. "If on every day, five out of those five thousand ideas were good, if you could figure out a way to throw those five back—'Okay, I got 'em all, and I think these twenty-five are best'—and you could figure out how to throw them back, and get responses, and figure out how to improve these, flesh them out, . . . you actually might, because it's so instanta-neous and it's so democratic, you might be able to actually set up a governance system around social media that's never been done before." It would be a new feedback loop.

San Francisco has just started to explore these kinds of feedback loops. The city has launched SFpark, a system to help drivers find parking spaces. Not only does the system collect real-time information on available parking; it also adjusts the costs of meters and parking garages to reflect demand. By creating this ongoing feedback loop, the city makes it easier to find free and affordable parking. SFpark, the first such program in the nation, makes it possible to "circle less and live more," as its Web site boasts.

We need more of these kinds of feedback loops, as they can help solve all kinds of problems. Here's another example: A few years ago, when San Francisco tried to create a bonus system for certain management levels, we ran into trouble. We needed to develop criteria for giving out bonuses, but this proved difficult, as the various players couldn't agree on what those criteria should be. What constituted success? And who should be the judge of whether a manager or department has achieved it?

Well, if you believe, as I do, that satisfaction of the consumer/constituent is the most reliable indicator of whether you're doing a good job, then there's an easy answer. Why not use feedback loops—Yelp-style reviews and comments—to determine performance bonuses? The purpose of government is to serve the people, after all. So if the people respond positively to your efforts, then you're probably doing your job well.

Moreover, we can use such feedback loops not only for external evaluations, but for internal ones as well. The customers of many government departments are actually other government departments. Why not set up an internal, interdepartmental feedback loop?

This type of feedback loop also helps solve a core problem of politics. The only time most politicians care about satisfying their constituents is—you guessed it—on election day. Historically, election day was the only day when constituents' feedback really mattered. Being a successful politician has always been defined by winning elections: If you win, you're a good politician. If you lose, you're not. And too often, after a politician wins an election, he or she suddenly shows little to no interest in what constituents want or need—outside of reading an occasional public-opinion poll to decide how to vote on an issue—until the next campaign season.

Those days are ending. With the ability to set up clear, clean, transparent feedback loops, we're finally leaving behind the one-way "we provide a service, and you take it or leave it" of Government 1.0. One-way is over, and two-way is in! We're leaving behind the vending machine and moving toward the cloud.

## . . . AND FABULOUS PRIZES!

The key to all of this—to game-based interaction, feedback loops, and social media—is getting people to participate. And there's one other proven way to get people to participate: by offering prizes.

"Have you heard of a guy named Victor Garcia?" Aneesh Chopra asked me. "He immigrated from Mexico at age five, and eventually was a community college enrollee who was waiting tables. He meandered from Texas to California, enrolled in a technical institute, and got an entry-level job at Peterbilt," the truck manufacturer. And that's where Garcia was working in early 2011 when he heard about a contest sponsored by the Defense Advanced Research Projects Agency (DARPA).

On February 3, 2011, DARPA launched something called the Experimental Crowd-Derived Combat Support Vehicle (XC2V) Design Challenge. The goal: to quickly develop a combat vehicle that could be used for reconnaissance as well as delivery and evacuation. Anyone could enter, and the winner—chosen by vote—would receive $7,500 in cash in addition to seeing his or her prototype built.

Normally, the process of developing this kind of vehicle would take forever and cost a fortune. There'd be a whole government procurement process, in which current contractors would have the edge, and for all the time and money spent, we'd end up with one design. But by creating a contest, DARPA ensured that there would be dozens of designs to choose from, none of which would cost the taxpayers a single penny.

More than 150 submissions came in, one of which was Victor Garcia's. Voting was open until March 10, and designers commented on each other's designs, offering suggestions for improvements. When all the votes were tallied, Garcia's Flypmode, a futuristic vehicle resembling some kind of Transformer, had won. Within fourteen weeks, a company called Local Motors built the prototype, which was then delivered, with keys, to President Obama in a ceremony.

This was unheard of—a brand-new combat vehicle, solicited, designed, and built in less than six months. As Chopra later said publicly, "[Garcia] was chosen, not because of his statement of purpose, but because he produced a product that according to his peers around the country was best in class. There are hidden pockets of innovation throughout this country. There are Victor Garcias in every neighborhood. This is what open government is all about."

So the question is—why not run contests like this all the time? Why not throw open the doors of innovation to anyone who feels they have something to offer? What exactly is the downside of a process that (a) results in a wider variety of choice, (b) costs less, and (c) takes less time than the current way of procuring innovative new designs? And the bonus is, these kinds of contests make people feel more engaged than ever with their government. "My instinct," Chopra told me, "is that you'll see more innovation in solving government priorities external to government apparatus than internal. That's why it's so important to pursue challenges, prizes, innovation. . . . We will solve the unsolvable through open innovation."

The Obama administration is in it to win it. In March 2010, the Office of Management and Budget (OMB) released a memo inviting departments and agencies to use contests for sparking innovation. The memo laid everything out, explaining potential policy hurdles and legal ramifications while urging agencies to "utilize prizes and challenges as tools for advancing open government, innovation, and the agency's mission."

The memo also promised that within 120 days, the administration would create a "Web-based platform for prizes and challenges." The result was Challenge.gov, a first-of-its-kind Web site where federal agencies can launch and publicize their contests. A quick scroll through Challenge.gov reveals a huge range of contests from agencies across the board, including:

- **Apps Against Abuse**, launched by the Department of Health and Human Services to create apps to help young adults to fight back against relationship violence and sexual assault;
- The **Bright Tomorrow Lighting Prize,** launched by the Department of Energy to speed the shift from inefficient old lighting products to new, high-performance ones;
- The **MyPlate Fruits and Veggies Video Challenge,** launched by the USDA to increase awareness of healthy diets;
- The **Absentee Voting Poster Contest,** launched by the Department of Defense to educate military personnel about absentee voting; and
- The **Mapping Dark Matter** contest, launched by NASA to aid in the mapping of this invisible component of the universe.

Prizes for these particular five contests range from $3,000 to $15 million, but the submissions roll in for all contests, regardless of how big or small the prize is. New ideas, citizen engagement, even the launch of brand-new industries—the US government's embrace of contests, aided by December 2010 legislation that expressly permitted them, has created a win-win for all involved. "Congress gave us the authority to run challenges and contests," Chopra told me, referring to the new law. This is good, he continued, because "I tend to think of procurement as evil—a machine unto itself." Creating challenges means we can sidestep the evils of procurement while simultaneously encouraging innovation.

Although few people know it, these kinds of government challenges actually have been around a long, long time—almost three hundred years, to be exact.


## THE LONGITUDE PRIZE

For centuries, sailors at sea knew how to calculate their latitude based on the positioning of the sun. But whenever a ship sailed out of view of land, no one had yet figured out how to calculate the longitude of its position. Hundreds of ships and thousands of sailors had been lost when voyages ended in shipwrecks, and the so-called longitude problem was, as X Prize founder Peter Diamandis notes, "the big issue of the day"—even to the extent that other big problems were sometimes described as being "as difficult as longitude."

Tired of losing sailors and ships, the British government in 1714 created the Longitude Prize—a £20,000 award (more than $4 million in today's money) for whoever discovered a method for calculating longitude to within thirty nautical miles. Anyone could enter, and the government also pledged awards to those who provided assistance that helped lead to an eventual solution.

The ultimate winner, to nearly everyone's surprise, was not an astronomer or navigator. He was a watchmaker named John Harrison, and he won by coming at the problem from a different angle than most. Harrison realized that the problem could be solved with a watch that kept accurate time at sea, where the waves, the winds, and the fluctuations in temperature and humidity threw off conventional timepieces. Harrison solved the problem by inventing the marine chronometer.

Unfortunately for Harrison, the British government and its Longitude Board seemed doubtful, if not dumbfounded, that a mere watchmaker had solved the problem. Harrison got paid only in fits and starts, never receiving the full £20,000 prize. He received £4,315 during the period from 1737 to 1764, and then another £10,000 in 1765, when he was sixty-eight years old.

Like Victor Garcia, who would otherwise never have had a chance to design a combat vehicle for DARPA, John Harrison would never have been given a chance to solve the longitude problem if it weren't for a government-sponsored incentive prize. One wonders how many other thorny problems could be solved by opening them up to everyone who has the time, energy, and inclination to try.

The history of such prizes repeats this pattern again and again: In 1795, Napoléon offered 12,000 francs to anyone who could create a food-preservation method so that French troops could carry food with them as they invaded Russia. The winner?—not a chemist or physicist but . . . a candy maker. In 1919, the Orteig Prize of $25,000 was offered to the first person to fly from New York to Paris nonstop. The winner? A relatively untested pilot named Charles Lindbergh—a man nicknamed the Flying Fool, who'd been flying for only about two years. No equipment company would sponsor him, as people were afraid he would crash and kill himself.

As Peter Diamandis has noted, these types of competitions result in much more than just the solution to a given problem. For the Orteig challenge, Diamandis told me, "Over eight years, nine different teams spent about $400,000 trying to win the $25,000 prize." And all of that $400,000 worth of research and development—paid for by the participants themselves, not the government or the sponsor of the prize or anyone else—led to modifications that further improved the nascent aviation industry.

Diamandis, an MIT-trained aerospace engineer (not to mention a Harvard MD), was so inspired by the story of the Orteig Prize that he decided to launch his own prize. As a child, he had dreamed about the day when ordinary citizens could buy tickets to fly into space. But as he got older, he realized that no one was seriously working on it—not NASA, which had other goals, and not private companies, for whom the cost of investment seemed too high. So he decided to take on the problem himself by creating an incentive prize similar to the Orteig Prize.

The winner, Diamandis decided, would have to "demonstrate a sub-orbital, private, fully reusable spaceship." He knew the prize had to be large because the competitors' investments would be significant. So in 1995, he set out to raise $10 million, never imagining it would take him six years to do so. He approached philanthropists and heads of companies, hoping to find someone to give a name to his prize, which he temporarily named the X Prize. In 2001, when he finally found his sponsors—Anousheh, Hamid, and Amir Ansari—he decided to keep the X in the name. And so the Ansari X Prize was born.

Just three years later, Mojave Aerospace Ventures launched a manned vehicle called SpaceShipOne sixty miles into the sky, landed it safely, and then repeated the journey. The unthinkable was now possible: The success of SpaceShipOne opened the door to private civilian travel into space. The Mojave Aerospace—a joint venture between tech billionaire Paul Allen and aerospace engineer Burt Rutan—collected the $10 million Ansari X Prize, which it had spent $25 million to win. And that was just a fraction of the more than $100 million spent by all twenty-six competitors.

Why spend $25 million to win $10 million? That seems a pretty poor return on investment, doesn't it? But within months, Richard Branson announced that his new company, Virgin Galactic, would license the SpaceShipOne technology for a new private spaceflight business—an immediate and potentially very lucrative revenue stream for the winners. Mojave Aerospace certainly felt the investment was worth it, either for competitive reasons or otherwise. And Peter Diamandis had found a way to make his childhood dream a reality.

The success of the Ansari X Prize spurred Diamandis to launch other such prizes with other sponsors. Tackling an array of twenty-first-century problems, the competitions include:

- The **Progressive Insurance Automotive X Prize,** aimed at creating a car that can get a hundred miles per gallon using a combination of gas and electric power;
- The **Qualcomm Tricorder X Prize,** for developing a portable wireless device that monitors and diagnoses your health conditions;
- The **Google Lunar X Prize,** for putting a working robot on the moon; and
- The **Wendy Schmidt Oil Cleanup X Challenge,** in response to the BP disaster off the Gulf Coast, aimed at finding better technology for cleaning up oil spills.

All of these prizes share common traits: They address problems of vast scale that would take millions or billions of dollars of government investment to solve, and the effort put forth to solve them has the potential to launch entire industries.

"If you have clarity about what the solution, the end point, is," Diamandis told me, "if you can say, 'Here's the goal, this is what we're measuring, and the first person to achieve this wins,' then you can back the entire field around the globe. . . . It's almost fixed-price science or engineering. You pay only the winner."

## SEARCHING FOR THE CURE, NOT THE BAND-AID

The biggest problem with government today is that we've set it up to *manage* problems, not solve them. Too often, people in government are more interested in maintaining the status quo, because that's how they maintain their jobs. But passing programs is not the same thing as solving problems. Too often, programs are just Band-Aids, not cures.

Incentive prizes are a perfect bipartisan solution: They solve problems, help people, and save money, thereby fulfilling goals that span the whole political spectrum. These are the kinds of solutions that both Democrats and Republicans can get behind on local, state, and national levels—they transcend partisan politics. And to its credit, the Obama administration has begun to embrace this approach.

Such incentives are also the antidote to problems like the Solyndra fiasco. In 2009, the solar-power company Solyndra received a $535 million loan guarantee from the White House in hopes that the company would create new jobs and spur growth in this critical industry. Two years later, Solyndra filed for Chapter 11 and laid off most of its employees, costing taxpayers millions of dollars in unpaid debts. The Obama administration was pilloried for having given Solyndra what critics said was preferential treatment. It was all the nightmares of procurement with the worst possible ending.

What if, instead of simply guaranteeing a loan to a single company, the US government had launched an X Prize–style competition instead? The outcome would obviously have been very different. Loans and government contracts reward connections, history, and perseverance. X Prize–style competitions reward just one thing: success. You cannot win an X Prize unless you successfully solve the problem on the table. Period.

Where in government—or even in large corporations—is anyone backing crazy ideas with a high probability of failure? The answer, historically, has been nowhere. In large organizations, you take the easy road and innovate incrementally. You play it safe. But sometimes, you need to aim for the greater reward by taking that crazy risk. The beauty of incentive prizes is this: The competitors take the crazy risks, and we get the rewards. If you have a hundred teams competing and ninety-nine fail, that's just fine—as long as that one team succeeds.

So what's the drawback? From a political perspective, the biggest one is this: If you offer a prize that anyone can win, you can't control whose congressional district it goes to. Elected officials like to have some say in where vast pots of money get allocated, and the wide-open nature of incentive prizes means there's no telling where the money will go or where a new industry may be born. But this is regionalism pure and simple. And in solving the major problems of our era, the good of the country has to outweigh the political needs of any elected official.

When a senior fellow at Resources for the Future named Molly K. Macauley testified in front of the House Committee on Science, she enumerated three potential drawbacks of government incentive prizes. First: "Government typically cannot commit to funding beyond a fiscal year, thus limiting the timing of the prize competition and cutting short the time that might be required for the technical achievement it awards." Fortunately, thanks to new laws encouraging government-sponsored contests, this is no longer an issue. As Diamandis notes, "America COMPETES [the America Creating Opportunities to Meaningfully Promote Excellence in Technology, Education, and Science Act of 2007] now allows agencies to have multiyear monies."

Macauley's second point was related to her first and is answered similarly: "Any uncertainty about whether the prize will actually be awarded due to government budgets or changes in administration will weaken if not eliminate incentives to compete." Yet if we set up contests as ongoing parts of agency budgets, this problem goes away. And many cities, including San Francisco, are now moving toward multiyear budgets and capital plans, which makes it easier to set up multiyear contests.

Finally, Macauley said, "Intellectual property rights to the achievement may need to reside with the competitor to induce participation, even though the taxpayer, by financing the prize, could fairly claim rights." This, of course, is true of any government-funded research and development; it's the reason I urged caution when the University of California Board of Regents discussed expanding its capacity to sell research results from our universities. But in my view, it's as important for government to act as a venture capitalist as it is for it to simply be a giant, lumbering procurement vehicle. If we need to find new ways to adjudicate who owns what, then that's a price we must be willing to pay.

Diamandis answered the point even more stridently. "This makes no sense," he told me. "There's something on the order of $10 billion a year spent on AIDS research and care, and vaccine attempts, and just dealing with medical problems. That's *$100 billion* over a decade. It's a huge amount of money. And these are sunk costs; we're paying them year after year. Why wouldn't you just put up a billion-dollar prize for the person who could come up with a vaccine? Or a cure? The company would make a ton of money, but the billion-dollar prize would go to the researcher who comes up with the cure. It goes to the person or team—not the company. Think about how many grad students would be dreaming about that at night. . . . A $1 billion AIDS prize that's paid to the innovator who provided a cure would save the US government $99 billion no matter who owned the intellectual property.

"You have to be clear that you're incentivizing the right thing," Diamandis said. "You get what you incentivize. So if you want to incentivize people to keep creating drugs that maintain but don't solve chronic diseases, great. AIDS is now a disease that has a large population of people who are getting lots of drugs that they pay money [for] year in and year out." If a company's main focus is the bottom line, that's a predictable, stable, lucrative place to be. If you're thinking of shareholders, it's easy to see why such companies would rather continue what they're doing rather than chase after a vaccine or cure.

"Ultimately, if you want to incentivize a cure or vaccine," Diamandis told me, "then incentivize that. You don't pay them unless they do it—but if they do it, it's worth tens of billions of dollars to the US government. . . . NASA, DARPA, and the Department of Energy are putting millions per year into prizes. So this is just noise for the government. It's a small amount."

But here's the best thing of all: The government doesn't even have to come up with the prize. Diamandis, for example, found the Ansari family, Qualcomm, Progressive Insurance, Google, and others to sponsor his X Prizes. "I don't get why the largest philanthropists—billionaire philanthropists—aren't saying, 'These are the top ten problems we have. And we're putting up a billion dollars—or a hundred million dollars, I don't know what the right number is—to solve each one," he told me. "I'd love to see five percent of all philanthropy done in the form of incentive prizes. It really challenges people to do bold and meaningful acts that are beneficial.

Incentive prizes aren't a panacea; they're not meant for everything," he said. "But where they do work well, they're great." And the reason is, they all rely on one of the most basic human drives, the drive to compete. People like to win, and they like others to know that they've won. So creating competitions in which people try to outdo one another—especially when those contests are waged in public—is a sure way to ramp up interest and participation.

"We are genetically bred to compete," says Peter Diamandis. "We do our best work when we're competing—in politics, in sports, in business, for your spouse. And so I'm trying to create a mechanism where we bring to bear people taking risks and going for it to solve grand challenges."

# EIGHT

# By the People, for the People

IN NOVEMBER 2000, people throughout the United States began seeing some strange photographs. Newspapers and TV stations showed middle-aged men and women hunched over, squinting intently at rectangular pieces of paper. Some looked cross-eyed, they were staring so hard. One famous photo showed a grayish, balding man holding a giant magnifying glass, peering through it with a bloodshot eye that looked three times its normal size.

These images of election workers and volunteers poring over ballots in Florida showed how embarrassingly primitive our voting system truly was. Here in the world's most powerful nation, we were choosing our president by asking people to stare at paper ballots, trying to sort out punched holes from not punched holes from semi-punched holes with "hanging chads." Our country's leadership hung in the balance, and all we could do was hope that a handful of tired people was counting our votes correctly.

A little more than two years later, Americans found themselves voting once again. But this time the process had been made far easier and more accessible. Now people could vote from the privacy of their own homes, by either calling an 800 number or sending a text message. Their votes were recorded by computer, and the results, announced the following week, were eagerly watched throughout the country.

This was a far more efficient way to vote, and millions of people—particularly young people—eagerly jumped to do it. And that's how the TV show *American Idol* became a smash hit. It made voting easy, and people believed their votes counted. They felt engaged, as they were making a difference in something they cared about—pretty much the opposite of how people feel in government elections.

We have a serious problem with voting in this country: People are less and less interested in doing it. The numbers have been dropping for decades—in the 1900 presidential election, the proportion of eligible voters who cast ballots was 73 percent. A hundred years later, in 2000, the number was just 51 percent. Even in a year when the electorate was unusually engaged—the 2008 contest, when Barack Obama's candidacy fired up both parties—the number stood at 57 percent.

Why the apathy? The reasons aren't too hard to figure out. People don't think their votes matter. They think the candidates aren't really that different, anyway—they're all politicians, after all!—so it doesn't really matter who gets into office. They're turned off by the inconvenience of voting. And they think politics is ruled by money and special interest groups. When you add these discouragements together, the sum total is, not surprising, indifference.

The question of money in elections grew even more contentious after the Supreme Court's *Citizens United* decision in 2010, which made it possible for corporations, unions, and private individuals to give unlimited sums of money to campaigns. The Court's decision led to an explosion of Super PACs—political action committees that collect hundreds of millions of dollars from those who want to influence the outcome of elections.

As John McCain told Jay Leno on *The Tonight Show*, this was "the worst decision of the United States Supreme Court; they should be ashamed and embarrassed at what they did." He went on to say, "I just wish one member of the Supreme Court had ever run for sheriff. They would understand that unlimited amounts of money [coming from] individuals, unions, corporations—whatever it is—is corruption."

The rise of the Super PACs also had one other consequence, according to veteran political strategist Simon Rosenberg: It has undercut the Internet's effectiveness as a fund-raising medium. "The reason the Democrats went to the Internet," he said, "was because high-end contributions couldn't be used for TV ads. . . . But now you can raise high-end money. So why engage middle-class people, when you can just engage fifty rich people?"

These problems undermine the very foundation of our government. After all, when nearly half the people in a representative democracy take no part in shaping it, and only a handful of very rich people are funding the candidates, can it really even be called a democracy anymore?

How can we fix this? Where do we begin? Let's go back to our basic premise: that we must use technology to help us solve our problems. So how can we use technology to bring voting from the nineteenth century into the twenty-first century?

## USING AN ABACUS WHEN WE HAVE CALCULATORS

Imagine for a moment that you just turned eighteen. Your whole life, you've been voting, rating, commenting, and otherwise influencing the world around you. You regularly post reviews to Yelp, you promote things you like on Pinterest, you designed your own sneakers at Nike.com, you vote every week on *American Idol*, you broadcast your whereabouts via Foursquare. Your smartphone is your lifeline to the world. You're used to having everything you need at the touch of a button, whether it's GPS or games or apps or the Internet.

And now, you're about to vote in a presidential election for the first time! This is the moment your eighth-grade American history teacher said would be a turning point in your life. It's the moment you finally get to take part in the great American system of government—that is, if you remembered to register to vote in time, because you have to do so in advance of the election.

On election day, you look at the booklet you received by snail mail to find your polling station. You realize you'd better get hopping, as it's only open during certain hours. You drive down to the local fire station and find a line of people waiting to get in. Once you get in the door, there's a folding table with paper signs saying A–G, H–R, and S–Z. You get in line according to last name and wait for your turn at the table.

Someone hands you a piece of paper and points you toward a row of little desks with dividers. At each desk, there's a machine you've never seen before. It's a machine that helps you color in the holes on your ballot. You dutifully line up your card and use the special pen to fill in your choices. This reminds you of the abacus you once saw in a history book. Sure, it does the job, but wouldn't you really rather use a calculator?

When you've finished voting, another person gives you an I VOTED sticker to wear. You leave the fire station and finally reenter the twenty-first century: You immediately whip out your phone to find a nearby café, check out its ratings, find an online coupon for a coffee and doughnut there, and locate a parking space nearby. It dawns on you that there's a serious disconnect between the world of voting and the real world. You peel off your I VOTED sticker and post the update "I Voted" to your Facebook page. Twenty-six friends click LIKE within ten minutes.

Yes, you have voted. And yes, your vote will be counted. But everything else about the voting experience can only be described as archaic. It's just another example of how government is far behind the private sector in adopting new technologies. And it's another reason why young people feel the language of government is a language they just don't understand.

Given the potential for fraud, developing a foolproof system for e-voting will take time. Many people have expressed very valid concerns—and of course, the number-one concern should always be guaranteeing the integrity of the election results. But electronic voting is already used in several countries, including Brazil, Switzerland, and Estonia. And direct-recording electronic (DRE) voting machines have been used sporadically in US elections, too, though paper ballots are still used in most elections. So creating and using a secure system for e-voting *is* a possibility, but it just hasn't been a priority in this country.

Our old friend E-stonia is on the forefront of this movement. In the 2011 parliamentary elections, fully 15 percent of Estonian voters cast their votes over the Internet. Not only that, but they could cast their votes during the week prior to election day. Rather than having to schlep down to a polling place within certain hours on a single day, Estonians could vote from the comfort of their own homes over a several-day period. We have entered an age when technology is enabling people to do whatever they want, whenever they want. Government, too, must offer that option.

In the United States, growing numbers of counties offer early voting options. Washington State offers a vote-by-mail option that also frees people from the constraints of election-day hours. And Oregon has begun experimenting with iPad voting. The initial project was limited: allowing voters with disabilities to vote by iPad to save them from the hardship of traveling to a polling place. Oregon's system wasn't perfect—the ballot then had to be printed and mailed rather than being electronically tabulated—but it was an important first step. Because when it takes less time and effort to start a blog, buy a new pair of shoes online, or even research the history of American elections than it does to actually cast a vote, we need to change that.

Simon Rosenberg echoed this view. "We have designed the least consumer-friendly voting process in the world. If we allowed people to vote over a three-day period, that would help. When you offer early voting, or voting from your living room, participation goes up. As people's lives get busier, they spend more time in the cars, and they don't take time to vote. The voting system in the US just hasn't kept up. . . . We're not giving people meaningful ways of engaging with political leaders."

But here's the kicker: We *do* know how to use technology to increase participation in government. We haven't done it for voting, but political campaigns have taken great pains to make one other experience—fund-raising—smoother and easier. When there's something politicians want from their constituents, they'll work to make sure they can get it.

"Fund-raising is the leading edge because it's very direct," said Eric Ries. "It's immediate." Campaigns are eagerly investigating every possible method for letting people give money, not only via the Internet, but also by text messaging. Yet we can't be satisfied with just improving the ways people can give money. We must put the same energy and effort into other forms of engagement, too.

So fix number one should be: Use technology to make voting easier. Let people use their phones or computers to vote without having to go to a physical place. And let them vote over a series of days, not just one day. This should be a high priority—not something we stumble toward while new generations grow more and more alienated from our democracy. In fact, the best thing we could do would be to host an X Prize–style competition to create that system. Let's offer a cash prize, throw open the doors to innovation, and see what people come up with. This is exactly the kind of problem we should be solving by big incentive prizes.

And voting is only the beginning. The real progress will come when we solve the problem of getting people engaged beyond just that one-day commitment to casting a ballot.

## THE MESSAGE: "YOU'RE A COUCH POTATO"

"It used to be that you could only participate in politics in two ways: Watch a TV ad and vote," Simon Rosenberg has observed. "There was no way into the system. The message was, 'You're a couch potato.'"

Now, says Rosenberg, people can play a true role beyond simply voting. "What do people want?" he asks. "They want their voices to be heard. How do you manage that? The offer of engagement must be real." So how do we make it real?

Let's start by looking at what doesn't work. Have you ever been to a city council meeting? Or a town-hall meeting? These are supposed to be shining examples of democracy—gatherings where ordinary people can come together, hear their elected officials speak, and ask them direct questions, make comments, or make requests. It's a very pretty picture of how democracy works. It's also easily stacked against ordinary citizens.

Here's what really happens: Activists and special interests pack these meetings with people on their side. They rent buses and sometimes even pay people to pile in to bring their numbers up. The loudest voices get the most attention, so the "debate" often devolves into shouting. Free exchange of ideas? Not exactly—more often than not this is little more than theater. Most people don't have time to come down to these meetings—they're putting their kids to bed or tending to a hundred other things. Town halls increasingly reflect little more than the views of a few special interests.

When I was mayor, I stopped doing traditional town-hall meetings, because the only people who showed up were the 24/7 special interests. I got pilloried for the "antidemocratic" move of shutting the doors on them—but the reality was that the traditional town halls themselves were antidemocratic. And perpetuating the fraud of true "public engagement" would have been far worse than admitting that it wasn't working.

I wanted to find ways for all to express their opinions equally, so we brought in new technology in the form of the AmericaSpeaks hand-held devices that allowed people to quietly vote on their priorities. Right away we saw improvements: We could ensure greater diversity of the participants, because attention didn't go merely to the loudest and most strident. We could facilitate deliberation more easily. These scaled-back meetings brought out more voices than we'd ever had, living up to their name, SF Listens.

I was glad to make an antidemocratic process a little bit more democratic. But the reality is, there was still only an infinitesimal number of people participating. I was proud of that progress, but deep down I knew it was still inadequate.

So the next thing I tried was doing town halls via telephone. We sent out robo calls saying, "Hi, if you'd like to participate in a live town hall now, please press one." We called thousands of households, but of course only a fraction took part.

Finally, we tried an Internet town hall. Two reporters moderated, and we spent nearly two hours in spirited discussion, using Facebook and Twitter as our platforms. People could send in any question or comment they wanted, in real time, and the reporters would pass them along. The whole thing was also televised live. Better, but still not good enough.

Twitter town halls, petition sites, SF Listens—these all fall into the category of "nice try, but we have to do better." All three of our alternative town halls were better than showing up at a traditional town-hall meeting and shouting to be heard, so we're moving in the right direction. But we've got to keep trying new things.


## THE LESSON OF CHANGE.GOV

How else can we get people engaged? People are so fed up these days that some are supporting a national referendum. Don't like the decisions your government is making? Putting referenda on the ballot lets the people vote directly on policies. Is this the answer?

Only in limited cases. Referenda prove how frustrated people are. They're the citizens' way of saying, "We can do better." And putting issues up for a popular vote can certainly get more people out for elections. Yet as with so many other elements of politics, special interests own the referendum process, too. Big, powerful, well-funded groups are often the driving force behind referenda, which cost a lot money to get on the ballot. Just like the town halls, the process of getting referenda on the ballot can squeeze out the little guy.

That can lead to other problems, as we saw here in California with Proposition 8, the referendum to take marriage rights away from same-sex couples. When Prop 8 came up for a vote in November 2008, gay men and lesbians had been able to marry legally for nearly five months. With Prop 8 on the ballot, people were voting to take away rights from a minority group by changing the state constitution—an unprecedented and unwelcome development. Prop 8 was an example of how insidious the referendum process can be.

In California, we've seen other ways in which the process can run amok. Hiram Johnson, who was governor in 1911 when California voters passed the state constitutional amendment establishing the initiative and referendum system, called it "a gun in the hand" of voters. The truth is, the referendum process has proven to be easily abused, and it has resulted in all kinds of unintended consequences—such as the majority voting to take away a civil right from a minority. One report on the initiative process declared that:

> Today, we could describe it as the initiative industrial complex, given the number of companies providing services such as signature-gathering, legal services, and campaign consulting that are now integral and apparently essential to the process. The days of romanticizing it as the "citizens" initiative process are long over.

So while referenda can sometimes be useful, they aren't the answer for how to get more people engaged and revitalize our democracy. But what other methods are there? What other ways have we tried to bring democracy into the twenty-first century?

In the days leading up to Barack Obama's inauguration, his transition team invited people to tell Obama which issue they wanted him to focus on first as president—the war in Iraq? Unemployment? Climate change? The housing crisis? People were asked to submit their ideas to the Web site Change.gov or simply vote for whichever issue they cared about most. Great idea, right? What better way to get people engaged and show them that the incoming president would take their concerns seriously? What could possibly go wrong?

Here's what. When Obama was inaugurated, the top issue on Change.gov was this: "Will you consider legalizing marijuana so that the government can regulate it, tax it, put age limits on it, and create millions of new jobs and create a billion-dollar industry right here in the US?" That's a real issue and a genuine question. But . . . fully seven of the top ten issues on Change.gov were about the exact same thing. The ballot box had been stuffed.

As author Clay Shirky observed about the Change.gov process, "It was almost custom-designed for hijacking by special interests." Once again an effort to provide a forum where everyone could be heard equally and where ordinary people could speak directly to power was turned into just another town-hall meeting where the screamers drowned out the rest of us. Special interests deserve to have their positions heard just as much as anyone else, of course—but not at the expense of others.

"The lesson of Change.gov is do not create a king-of-the-hill system in which one group of citizens with one kind of issue has to outshout others to be heard," Shirky told me. "The design of the system overprivileged small groups of coordinated actors versus larger, more diffuse groups of citizens." For its part, the Obama administration pulled back from the notion that the president would address whichever Change.gov issue was on top. "That was just about the last time they tried to use these tools to govern, not just to campaign," said Shirky. "There was a sense of, 'Oh, god! Don't open that lid again!'"

These are some of the myriad ways that we've tried and failed to truly engage people in governing—and they all seem to have a common thread. Instead of allowing people to truly make their voices heard, they simply provide a platform for special interests to hijack the system. Are there ways to create genuine civic participation without repeating those same patterns? Yes there are—and they're coming from a place you might not expect.


## THE GOP AND TWITTER

When people think of politicians on the cutting edge of technology, they don't necessarily think of Republicans—but they should, because some of the most innovative and forward-thinking projects today are originating on the GOP's side of the aisle. This is no accident. After getting badly outplayed in the technology and social-media spheres in the 2008 campaign, Republicans knew they had to catch up. Barack Obama's campaign had skillfully used Facebook, YouTube, and Twitter to drum up support while John McCain's campaign lagged far behind. For the Republicans to have any hope of being relevant in the tech age, they would have to learn how to use these new tools effectively.

At a Republican retreat following the election, House Speaker John Boehner led the charge. An October 2011 *New York Times* story set the scene:

> At a January 2009 retreat, as defeated Republicans licked their wounds, Mr. Boehner told his colleagues that they needed to "think about the potential of new media," according to a copy of his remarks. He urged members and their staff to immediately get themselves on YouTube and Twitter, as he did. Without control of the House floor, it became the Republicans' main messaging tool as they mounted their successful push to capture control of the House. Now, it is their weapon of repetition.

Boehner's call to arms changed the whole game. Republicans took his advice in droves, as the *Times* went on to report:

> Republican House members have more than twice as many followers as their Democratic counterparts—about 1.3 million versus roughly 600,000—and are far more active on Twitter with more than 157,000 individual Twitter messages, versus roughly 62,000 for Democrats.

This is a remarkable turnaround, one that bodes well not only for Republicans but for all of us. Any time Republicans set the standard for something, we Democrats will naturally try to up our game—so the true winners, of course, are the constituents. In a competition between parties for who can be the most open and communicative, everyone wins.

Majority leader Eric Cantor is the man to watch in this new generation of tech-savvy Republicans. With his new-media guru, Matt Lira, guiding the way, Cantor is redefining the notion of "civic engagement" through new projects on his MajorityLeader.gov Web site. The first, launched in May 2010, was a program called YouCut.

"YouCut is a Web site with three to five items each week that people could vote for to try to cut wasteful spending," Lira told me. "It's a million-dollar hammer." People could cast votes online or via cell phone for items they'd like to see eliminated from the federal budget—anything from wasteful programs to unnecessary purchases. At the end of each week, Majority Leader Cantor would submit whichever item got the most votes to the full House for an up-or-down vote on whether to eliminate it.

Cantor did this every week, tallying the YouCut votes on Wednesday and bringing the item to the House floor on Friday. This was no mere opinion poll, designed just to let people vent. This was a commitment to let people have a real say in how their money was being spent. As majority leader, Cantor was guaranteed one vote a week—and he chose to give that vote to the people. Every single week.

"Everything was designed to validate people's decision to participate," Lira told me. And it worked: In YouCut's very first week, seven hundred thousand people voted. That high rate has continued into the broadened YouCut Phase II, which was launched in March 2011—each week between five hundred thousand and a million people vote.

"Anytime we ask people to do something online, I want it to have real impact on the process," Lira told me. "I call this the 'realness rule.' I want to find ways to bring people through the system in ways that can have genuine impact on the process." YouCut is the antidote to a system where, most often, people are invited to submit their opinions and comments online for one purpose: so that elected officials and campaigns can build up their mailing lists for future fund-raising. The question, says Lira, is "How can we incorporate social media into the act of governing itself—not just as a communications device. The key to that is participation."

## PROJECT MADISON

Representative Darrell Issa is another Republican on the front lines of this fight. In early 2012, Issa fought against the Stop Online Piracy Act (SOPA), legislation that many believed would inhibit Internet freedom. In response, he introduced an alternative bill called the Online Protection and Enforcement of Digital Trade (OPEN) Act. But instead of simply drafting the bill for submission, he decided to invite people to take part in crafting the legislation.

He dubbed the effort Project Madison and launched a Web site—KeepTheWebOPEN.com—where anyone could offer comments and edits. This was unheard of. Normally, legislation is drafted behind closed doors on Capitol Hill, and constituents get to see only the finished product, not all the drafts and revisions. But Issa wanted, as journalist Greg Ferenstein wrote in *Fast Company*, to invite "the legions of angry technology firms and policy wonks to construct their own version" of the bill.

Ferenstein described how the site was set up:

> Project Madison is a stripped-down interactive blogging platform, which allows citizens to select individual passages of legislation, and strike or add their own language, with comments for each suggestion. Citizens are encouraged to like or dislike each change, with the most popular suggestions rising to the top. Each page also has embedded Facebook and Twitter buttons that link to individual amendments.

How's that for a new way of engaging people in government? Instead of simply sending out a one-way e-mail blast to announce an upcoming, already written bill, why not invite people to actually take part in writing it? If we want people to feel some ownership over the government process, after all, letting them take part in creating legislation is a pretty great way to do so.

And lest you think that Project Madison was just window dressing—a way for Representative Issa to look like the good guy while his staff just submitted the bill they wanted to submit—the Web site listed every change that was ultimately incorporated into the bill's language. The staff even wrote up a short "rationale" for why each change was included. Every step of the process, from start to finish, was absolutely transparent.

That transparency extended beyond the changes themselves to the identities of who suggested them. Behind the closed doors of Capitol Hill, lobbyists are constantly influencing and even drafting legislation—and you and I never know about it. But on the Project Madison site, anyone can see who is making the proposed changes. No secrets, no surprises.

So why not extend this idea to other legislation as well? Matt Lira singled out the health-care debate as a "huge opportunity to engage people. . . . Why couldn't you have a platform where every nurse in America goes to a Web page that says, 'Here are the two pages [of the legislation] that affect nurses in America. What do you think?' People will engage in that if it's targeted to niche audiences."

Let's open up the legislative process beyond just letting people call or write letters to their representatives. Let's make it possible for people to truly take part. "The standard," says Lira, "is to have direct citizen participation in all legislative matters, using communities that are already built in social networks. Everyone knows the Internet can effectively organize people *against* something, but I believe the real potential of social media will be its ability to organize people to *build* things." We have the technology, and it works. So let's use it.

## CITIZEN COSPONSORS

Six months after I sat down with Matt Lira in San Francisco, he sent me an e-mail telling me about a new project coming out of Majority Leader Cantor's office:

Today, we launched Citizen CoSponsors—a new program to enable constituents to cosponsor legislation that they support; in turn, they

will receive automatic updates as the bill moves through the legislative process and opportunities to participate in hearings, conference
call discussions, etc.

Once again, Cantor's office was paving the way for people to take a
substantive part in House business. But even better was the news of
how the Citizen CoSponsors program would work. As Lira wrote:

> It is built entirely on Facebook's Open Graph protocol, so updates
> can go to an individual's timeline, ticker, and news feed—right next
> to all the other daily updates they experience in their everyday life.

This is important for exactly the reason Lira stipulates: The updates
will appear on Facebook, right alongside a person's everyday-life
updates. One of the biggest hurdles in getting people excited about
government is overcoming this pervasive notion that government is
somehow separate from everyday life. A program such as this, where
updates from the House floor are interspersed with updates about your
friend's new dog or your sister's birthday party, is actually a huge step
toward making government a normal, everyday part of life.

Like Representative Issa's Project Madison, Citizen CoSponsors
will allow people to take a much larger part in crafting legislation. Lira
described how it works: "The first level empowers people with the
ability to follow the specific legislation that they care about, without
having to step outside of their existing daily habits. The next level will
engage communities in the actual legislative process to substantively
improve the policy outcomes."

More specifically, here's the kind of thing that Citizen CoSponsors
makes possible: Imagine teachers and parents being able to substantively participate in the legislative process on an education bill. No

longer limited to simply watching on television, they will be able to ask questions at real hearings, offer feedback on specific legislative text, and talk with policy makers directly about their concerns. These are the kinds of shifts that social media make possible—and not only possible, but inevitable.

It may be hard to imagine now, but within this next decade, people will begin participating in government in all kinds of new ways. Technology is shifting power away from central institutions and into the hands of people, and programs like YouCut and Citizen CoSponsors are heralds of this new era of true participation—an era that's coming whether we in government like it or not.

This same upheaval has already happened in other major industries. Consider, for example, the field of journalism. Fifteen years ago, newspapers were a one-way information flow. Writers and editors put out stories, and readers read them. But with the advent of the Web, which led to a twenty-four-hour news cycle, newspapers suddenly found themselves shorthanded. It was one thing to put out a paper every morning. It was quite another to have enough reporters to put out a twenty-four-hour, nonstop news product.

The newspapers didn't have enough money to hire more people, so where would all this content come from? The answer, which many papers resisted for as long as they could, was readers. On just about every newspaper's Web site and on sites like the *Huffington Post* and AOL's Patch.com, you see invitations for readers to send in photos and written accounts of breaking news events, news tips, comments, and reviews. The readers have become the reporters because technology led inevitably to that outcome. One-way is dead.

No one foresaw that sea change for newspapers, but in hindsight it had to happen. The same is true for government. It's hard to predict exactly how this will unfold, but it's absolutely inevitable that the relationship between people and government will change. If nothing else, the changing expectations of new generations, weaned on smartphones and the Internet, guarantee that we can't just continue with business as usual.

## UPDATING THAT OLD TOWN HALL

Now let's revisit the question of those pesky town halls. We already know the problems: Having set times and locations is inconvenient; the discussion is often hijacked by special interests; and it's hard for people to make their voices heard. How can we use technology to get around these problems? We don't want to abolish the notion of town halls, but how can we augment them?

The answer lies in sites such as Quora.com. Founded by a couple of former Facebook employees, Quora.com is a question-and-answer Web site where people can discuss governmental and political issues. Anyone who's registered to the site can ask a question, and others chime in with answers or rate others' answers or offer edits to other answers. It's an ongoing, real-time discussion of the issues, where each person's voice is given equal weight.

On many Web sites, users' comment sections often devolve into crazy flame wars. That doesn't happen on Quora.com, in part because the site requires people to sign up using their real names rather than screen names. Also, unlike real-life town halls, the best way to have your answers heard is not by shouting the loudest. It's by having the best answers. An algorithm built into Quora.com allows users to rate each others' answers; if yours are deemed better than others', they'll be assigned greater value and have greater visibility. Quora .com rewards quality, not volume.

But the real beauty of how Quora.com works is that whatever question you ask may well be answered by someone who has unique knowledge of the topic. So for example, one of the questions on Quora.com was "Why did Eric Cantor kill the STOCK [Stop Trading on Congressional Knowledge] Act?" Several users responded, some of them offering speculation based on things they'd read or heard. But the top-rated answer came from . . . Eric Cantor. He is a member, along with many other movers and shakers in the fields of politics, science, technology, books, and the other topics Quora.com offers.

Another site, Localocracy, also offers the promise of town halls without the drawbacks. Founded in 2008 by a recent college graduate named Conor White-Sullivan and purchased in 2011 by the *Huffington Post*, Localocracy was envisioned as an online platform for political participation, a way for citizens to interact with their government and among themselves. It's geared toward communities—hence the name—and is intended as a way for people to solve specific community issues.

Thanks to its real-names-only policy, Localocracy can offer the pros and cons of numerous issues, side by side, without the flaming rhetoric of anonymous commenters. People can easily assess what community leaders, politicians, and citizens think about certain issues, without the shout-downs typical of real-life town halls. It also allows users to "recruit" answers from their local representatives to answer specific questions. The goal, according to White-Sullivan, is for Localocracy to "take politics from a world of promises to a world of participation."

Using technology to increase people's civic participation is the promise of our new hyperconnected world. In the same way that Wikipedia re-created the notion of what an encyclopedia was and in the same way that Facebook rewrote the rules on how we stay in touch with each other, sites like Quora.com and Localocracy can recast the way we communicate with each other on important civic issues.

These sites succeed in part because they're easy to use, but there have been other, similar sites that have failed because they were too complex, or buggy, or their interfaces were confusing. America Speaking Out—also launched by House Republicans—was one such example. It was meant to be an online town-hall platform where people could suggest policy ideas and vote on each other's suggestions. Unfortunately, the site was buggy, and there were too many fields to fill in and levels to get through. In fact, so many government Web sites on both sides of the aisle have been poorly designed that the Sunlight Foundation had a regular blog series to point them out and offer suggested redesigns.

If we in government want people to engage on our Web sites, we have to make them as usable and simple as commercial Web sites. Otherwise, people will get bored or frustrated and just click over to another site. This is a wake-up call, especially for the Democrats, who are getting their clocks cleaned by Republicans right now on all these new technologies. There's always something fun, easy, entertaining, or enlightening to do on the Web. We can't expect people to engage if we don't offer them the ease of use they're accustomed to.

## FOLLOWING THE REALNESS RULE

We also have to realize that people don't want to engage without purpose. We have to play by the realness rule, as people will no longer fall for promises of "participation" that are more cosmetic than real—promises such as online petitions.

"The level of savvy seems like it's going up," says Eric Ries, the author of *The Lean Startup.* "Even five years ago, people were saying, 'The Internet will change things.' But it was very much like, you'd do an online petition, but no politicians look at online petitions, so it doesn't matter. The Electronic Frontier Foundation used to have an action center, where you could send e-mails to your congressman about issues, but it felt like nothing ever happened as a result of that, so I got disheartened and *less* engaged. Like, this is a waste of my time, because it's not working! These bad laws are getting passed anyway."

To be fair, petition sites have some worth, in that they offer constituents a clear-cut way of communicating their concerns to those in power. But after that, just as with the town halls, the people in power have no obligation to do anything. It's all "Thanks for coming! See you next time!" and then nothing gets done. The truth of the matter is, even in the age of technology, a handwritten, snail-mailed letter still carries great weight, in part because it's such a rarity. One individually crafted letter is still worth dozens of electronically generated, identical letters.

The Web site Votizen.com tried to merge the best of both worlds: It went through a phase in which you could tweet or post an opinion and Votizen would print it out on actual paper and mail it to your representatives. "It's a translation from the high-tech world your customers live in to the paper-based, slow-moving, vanity-metrics-oriented world that you live in," said Eric Ries. "It's physically delivering a stack of paper." Is this the future of technology? Obviously not—which means that we in government have to find better ways of weighing our constituents' opinions.

Votizen has since launched new initiatives, bringing them into the forefront by using social media for campaigns and voting, but the effort to bring technology into actual governance continues. "We have to make the whole system more real-time, more transparent," says Ries. Sites like Quora.com are leading the way.

## THE BUDGET AND YOU

Here in California, where we have the ninth-largest economy in the world and a crushing deficit, the Web site BudgetChallenge.org offers people their chance to balance the budget on their own terms. Anyone visiting the site is invited to make decisions on how we spend and raise money.

If you were in charge, would you reduce the K–12 school year by ten days, which would save $2.4 billion but leave California's per-pupil spending far below the national average? Or would you add $6.4 billion to the education budget, which would *still* leave our per-pupil spending at 7 percent below the national average? Would you reduce services for the developmentally disabled to save $200 million? Would you reduce funding to California's state universities in order to save taxpayers money? Or would you increase it, to save students and their families from facing yet another tuition increase?

Difficult questions, difficult choices—California's budget crisis is real, and people should have a say in how we resolve it. Cutting programs always results in hardships, and raising taxes is no easier. But if we do neither, the budget crisis will only get worse. BudgetChallenge .org lets you make these decisions and then gives you the option of forwarding your choices to your elected officials. It's a way of making your voice heard.

And yet it falls short of the realness rule, doesn't it? Sure, you can send your budget choices along to your representatives, but they don't have to do anything about them; they don't even have to look at them, truth be told. How can we make the budget challenge into something more substantive, something more real?

We can do that by following the example of New York City and Chicago, where a few innovative city officials have implemented participatory budgeting. In 2011, residents of four New York districts were invited to take direct part in deciding how nearly $6 million of their council members' funds were allocated. Any resident eighteen or older could vote for items in the discretionary fund—things like installing a new band gazebo, adding more public trash cans, installing security cameras, and providing running water to a dog park. People could make real decisions about how real money was spent.

This kind of participatory budgeting had its start in Brazil in the late 1980s, and it has been evolving there ever since. In the city of Pôrto Alegre, officials allowed citizens to go online and vote on items that comprised a full quarter of the budget. And in the town of Ipatinga, officials made it possible for people to take part in budgeting not only through the Internet, but also by texting on their phones.

Do people really care about budgeting? You bet they do. One Brazilian state of 11 million people offered its citizens the chance to decide $93 million of budget items online. In eighteen hours, 1.2 million people voted. What's more, the World Cup was going on at the same time, and while most of the trending Twitter topics had to do with soccer, the budget was near the top of the list.

There are still kinks to be worked out in participatory budgeting. As writer Elizabeth Whitman noted in the *Nation* magazine:

In New York City, even a proposal that wins the majority of residents' votes is not a guarantee that residents' ideas will come to fruition. . . . This issue and several others highlight the double-edged nature of participatory budgeting. Indeed, within the academic microcosm of participatory budgeting, experts are as wary of its risks and limitations as they are optimistic about its potential.

And yet the drawbacks of such budgeting, in my opinion, don't come close to outweighing the benefits. In the four New York districts where citizens had a say in the budget, people invested significant time and energy in making their decisions. According to a report by the Community Development Project of the Urban Justice Center cited on BillMoyers.com, "approximately 6,000 voters cast ballots on which projects to fund. Nearly half of those voters had never been active in community issues before participatory budgeting." And a bonus: "In the overall effort, people of color and low-income residents were represented at higher rates than in traditional electoral politics."

These are exactly the kinds of initiatives we need now. With advances in feedback loops and social-networking technology, they're easier than ever to set up and maintain—and expand. As Gianpaolo Baiocchi, a Brown University professor who studies participatory budgeting, was quoted in the *Nation*, "The challenge is to use the discretionary funds as a stepping stone toward other kinds of decision making. Imagine how transformative it would be to actually control the way the city works and runs!" Transformative indeed—it would be a revolution, a transfer of power from the centralized government to the people the likes of which we haven't seen before.

# NINE

# Armies of Davids

A CONFESSION: I kind of like the Tea Party. I don't agree with its politics—particularly of its fringe elements—but I love anyone who gets involved the way they do. Hats off to the people who give enough of a damn to actually show up and try to take part in the business of governing, working to get their candidates elected and change the face of Congress rather than just sitting back and complaining about everything.

Many of my fellow Democrats have been dismissive of the Tea Party—a kind of "how dare they!" attitude that serves only to elevate the other side. It's one thing to object to what many of the Tea Partiers are saying, but it's another thing when some Democrats actually complain about people dressing up, marching with picket signs, and using the power of their numbers to effect change in Washington, as that's straight out of the Democratic playbook. Historically we've been the ones doing the chanting, the sit-ins, the organized arrests, the taking over of town halls. But when the Tea Partiers started doing the same thing, many Democrats protested, "Oh, no! This is not democracy! What are these people doing?" Our party demonstrated an unbelievably thin skin, and the more dismissive we were of the Tea Party, the more inflamed they became. The truth is, we deserve the Tea Party, because in many ways we helped create it.

The Tea Party, the civil rights movement, Occupy Wall Street, the Million Man March, Glenn Beck's Restoring Honor rally, Jon Stewart's Rally to Restore Sanity—these are just different sides of the same coin. They are movements of people who want to take back some control, to have their say in government. Even Stewart Brand, a progressive firebrand if ever there was one, expressed an affinity with the Tea Party when he told me, "I want government fixed, and the Tea Partiers want government fixed. . . . They take government seriously, and lots of people don't."

That kind of self-motivation is more critical than ever, because there are plenty of people in government who would really rather *not* hear from you—except when fund-raising or soliciting votes. You know the cycle: When an election is coming up, you get all kinds of mailings, calls, e-mails, and tweets. Then as soon as the votes have been cast, it's radio silence once again. Candidates are always happy to listen to voters' concerns. But the minute the election is over, they'd rather avoid the bother.

For many government entities, the mark of a great meeting is when no one shows up for public comment. As Ted Gaebler, the coauthor of the groundbreaking 1992 book *Reinventing Government*, told me, "We've changed the agenda [at meetings] to put citizen comment first, rather than last. . . . The net effect of people having enough time to discuss items they want to discuss and having all the ceremonial things— the Boy Scouts come at the beginning of the meeting at five thirty, the people who are getting awards, all the feel-good stuff, the pledge of allegiance—and by six thirty, those people have all gone home to dinner. And the serious people are there . . . and they have enough time to discuss their items. And they feel heard. They don't feel rushed. The net result is that we have relatively few people coming to our meetings," he went on. "We seat a hundred, and if we have five or ten after the ceremonial thing, that's a big crowd." I asked him if this was a good thing, and he said, "Well, that's what I'm wondering. We have an *efficient* government. There's no nonsense. But we don't do a lot of citizen outreach, though some of our departments do." So it's more efficient, more effective, but less engaged—and that, unfortunately, is undemocratic.

For elected officials, every time a citizen makes a complaint or request, it just feels like one more burden on an already busy schedule. It's understandable why they might feel this way, but that doesn't make it right. In fact, the more actively engaged citizens are, the closer we come to the original vision of the Founding Fathers. I don't mean to sound like a Tea Partier myself, but aren't these the principles our country was built on? Benjamin Franklin set up our first volunteer fire department. Volunteers raised money and took up arms in the Revolutionary War. Throughout the country, people took an active part, whether formally or informally, in the running of their towns—a kind of bottom-up democracy that served to strengthen the new nation.

"If you go back to the Founding Fathers, you realize, 'Oh yeah, government was very small.' You go back to volunteer fire departments, to mutual insurance companies, to subscription libraries. . . . But now we've created—government is like this special category of thing," Tim O'Reilly told me. "As opposed to, it's a set of things we do for each other." We've gotten very far away from that notion in recent decades, a trend we'd do well to reverse.

"It would be really worthwhile to do an inventory of what kinds of things are done better by people doing them themselves" as opposed to government, O'Reilly went on. "Using the iPhone analogy"—in which ordinary people created the iPhone apps that Apple ultimately sold—"what could government do to greatly expand the scope of action for citizens with respect to government programs?" How do we make it possible—through apps, Web sites, social networking, or whatever—for people to take greater part in governing?

Well, here's a radical thought: Maybe it's not up to those of us in government to make this happen. Maybe people should simply grab that power back rather than waiting for us to make it possible for them. In some ways, this process has already started.

## THE AGE OF AMATEURS

Glenn Reynolds was a University of Tennessee law professor when he launched a political blog called *Instapundit* in the summer of 2001. Blogs were the newest blip on the Web's radar then, and in the beginning, *Instapundit* had just a few hundred readers a day. That number began growing exponentially after September 11, 2001, and a decade later, *Instapundit* was getting more than 10 million page visits every month.

The success of his blog and the spectacular rise of blogging in general struck Reynolds as a cultural shift, the "triumph of personal technology over mass technology," as he put it. With blogging, the power of news and opinion no longer resided solely in the big institutions of mainstream media. One voice, emanating from a suburban bedroom, could launch a movement, even change the world.

That same power shift was happening in other big institutions, too—in companies, political parties, and governments. Small was the new big. Thanks to the Internet, the power of individual people was on the rise. Reynolds gave this phenomenon a name in his 2006 book, *An Army of Davids*. From the introduction:

We're accustomed to thinking that big organizations are the important organizations because that's how it's been in recent centuries. Starting around 1700, big organizations became the most efficient way to do a lot of things. . . . Keeping track of information required armies of clerks, secretaries, etc., who needed a big organization to support them. These concepts—which economists call "economies of scope and scale"—favored big organizations. Big companies, big governments, whatever. Mass production. Bigger was better. *Goliath rules.*

These had always been the truisms of history—that might makes right and power rests with those who are big enough to defend it. It all made perfect sense until the digital age came along.

Reynolds went on:

The growth of computers, the Internet, and niche marketing means that you don't have to be a Goliath to get along. Like David's sling, these new technologies empower the little guy to compete more effectively. They have, in fact, spawned a veritable army of Davids, now busily competing with Goliaths in all sorts of fields. . . .

In the future, the efforts of individuals and small groups, acting sometimes on their own and sometimes in informal cooperation with others, are likely to make a bigger difference than they've made in centuries.

I talked about this idea with Joe Trippi, who's famous for having organized his own army of Davids. Trippi orchestrated the grassroots fund-raising campaign for Howard Dean in 2004—the first presidential campaign to tap into the vast fund-raising potential of ordinary citizens. These days, Trippi sees armies of Davids rising up everywhere.

"Here's a great example," he said. "Think about Goliath as the recording industry: You always had to buy the whole album even though every song but one sucks. Then think about the army of Davids who began using Napster to rip songs. The more pushback they got, the more they broke the law." With so many people changing the rules to suit themselves, Goliath began staggering. Eventually, the record industry realized that this ragtag army of Davids had the potential to kill its giant business.

What happened next, of course, is the stuff of legend. As Trippi put it, "Apple says, 'We have an army of Davids. The slingshots are iTunes and iPods.'" Steve Jobs saw his opportunity and pounced: He grasped that the power of a big industry was no match for the power of millions of people demanding change. Some observers were surprised that the recording industry made the iTunes deal—but what other choice did they have? It was either make that deal or watch their business collapse under illegal downloads.

"The whole idea is the shift of power," said Trippi. "Armies of Davids organize themselves. And this power shifting is happening because we've all grown up in a communications environment." Before, there was no way to quickly and easily organize such an army. Now it's literally as easy as tweeting or posting to Facebook.

People can communicate, organize, incite. They can even overthrow governments, as we saw in Egypt, Tunisia, Libya, and Yemen during the Arab Spring. Social-networking sites fueled the uprisings in all these countries; Twitter and Facebook made it much easier for people to band together and act. And while it's true that, as Malcolm Gladwell has pointed out, people organized protests and revolutions just fine throughout pretechnological history, there's no doubt that these new technologies have sped up the process and concentrated power more easily into the hands of the people.

We've seen this kind of "people power" at work closer to home, too. After a social-media-fueled firestorm, the Susan G. Komen Foundation reversed its decision to cut off Planned Parenthood grants. After Wikipedia, Reddit, and other influential Web sites went dark in protest against the Stop Online Piracy Act, the US House of Representatives put off voting on the legislation. After Twitter and Facebook blew up with denunciations, Rush Limbaugh retracted his comments labeling Georgetown University Law School student Sandra Fluke a "slut."

These are just the beginning. The power of technology allows people to organize more quickly, more widely, and more cheaply than ever before. It has launched us into the Age of Amateurs, as it's called by the writer David Brin—a time when traditional authority is seeing its power erode under the onslaught of these armies of David.

## THE SAVING GRACE

Social media, Al Gore told me, is "a saving grace for democracy"—a belief he formed by looking far back into history. In his 2008 book, *Assault on Reason,* Gore wrote about the birth of representative democracy, which started with the printing press. "Five hundred years ago," Gore told me, "the printing press disrupted the medieval world order, in which monarchs, the Church, and feudal lords controlled everything. They controlled access to libraries, where there were books only monks could understand. People were illiterate, and powerlessness came from that."

The introduction of the printing press changed everything. "In two generations, it led to the Reformation, peasant revolt in Europe, and demands for self-governance. When people had access to the same information as the elites had controlled, they realized they could do a much better job governing themselves." They organized a new public square, where "information became an alternate source of power." The printing press was the medieval Facebook, empowering ordinary citizens—yet the balance of power would eventually shift back.

Centuries later, said Gore, when technology moved on, "television disrupted print." Once again, information was being controlled by elites, or as Gore put it, "The public square was controlled by gatekeepers." People's attention then shifted in large numbers to the one-way medium of television.

"Thomas Paine could walk out his front door and find low-cost printing places," Gore told me. "Barriers to entry were low for individuals. The quality of ideas and expression became a substitute for wealth and power." In print, anyone could enter the fray. But with broadcast television, that model was disrupted, because the only people on television were those who could afford to be on television.

Then along came the Internet. "It is the saving grace, potentially," said Gore, "because it will eventually displace broadcasting. In the words of the novelist William Gibson, 'TV will sink into the digital universe.' That's not happening quickly because the amount of broadband required for video is so large." But it is happening. "Social media empowers the connecting of citizens to one another. . . . The Internet mimics print in that it has low entry barriers for individuals," said Gore.

"Now you get individual bloggers changing the nature of the dialogue," says Gore. "As that begins to shift, as broadband becomes more widely available, as people get smartphones and tablets, their ability to reestablish a reason-based self-governance system is growing. . . . The empowering of individuals with information and the ability to connect with others of like mind is likely to be an unstoppable force."

# A WORLD OF PEOPLE CONTROL

All over the world, people power is on the rise. The prime minister of the United Kingdom, David Cameron, described his own vision of a peoplecentric new era in a 2010 TED talk. "There are three passages of history," Cameron said. "We have gone from a world of local control, then we went to a world of central control, and now we're in a world of people control."

In the age of local control, most of human history, people paid heed to their town or tribal leaders, because there were no means of fast communication or travel. In the industrial age, governments began wielding much greater power: Faster transport, telecommunications, and the rise of mass media made it possible for a central authority to exert real control.

Today, says Cameron, we are entering the age of genuine people power. "One hundred years ago," he noted, "sending ten words cost $50." Information was power, and it was expensive and difficult to obtain. Now we can send and receive unlimited information, and anyone in the world can have access to the whole history of human knowledge, as long as he or she has a Web-ready device. And with the advent of smartphones the time is soon coming when that number really will include everyone on earth.

There's no better evidence for this trend than the BBC story making the rounds in March 2012: "India Census: Half of Homes Have Phones but No Toilets." Yes, that's right—as of 2011, more Indians owned cell phones (63.2 percent) than had toilets in their homes (46.9 percent).

These devices are no longer considered luxury items; they are getting cheaper, faster, and more ubiquitous by the day. They are changing the way people interact, learn, and communicate. And that will change the nature of power forever by eliminating the layers of bureaucracy that have long stood in the way of true progress.

## IT'S TURTLES ALL THE WAY DOWN

In his 1988 book *A Brief History of Time*, Stephen Hawking told a funny story about an old woman at an astronomy lecture. The lecturer describes how the Earth orbits the sun, the sun orbits around other stars, and the whole universe is ordered around this essential truth. The woman, Hawking wrote, stands up and says, "What you have told us is rubbish. The world is really a flat plate supported on the back of a giant tortoise."

"What is the tortoise standing on?" the lecturer asks with a smirk.

"You're very clever, young man, very clever," the woman says, "but it's turtles all the way down!"

I'm reminded of this story sometimes when confronted with the innumerable layers of bureaucracy in government. We have managers of managers, supervisors of supervisors, and enough committees, subcommittees, groups, and subgroups to make a bureaucrat's head spin. It truly is "turtles all the way down."

That's completely unnecessary in this technological age. Our government is clogged with a dense layer of bureaucracy, a holdover from an earlier era that adds bloat and expense. It's like a clay layer, a filler that serves only to slow everything down. But technology can get rid of that clay layer by making it possible for people to bypass the usual bureaucratic morass.

Technology allows us to disintermediate—a word I love, even though it sounds torturous. To disintermediate just means to get rid of the middleman. Technology empowers the end user, allowing you to break through the clay layer—to break the business-as-usual, standard-operating-procedure, nine-to-five mentality that so afflicts government today. It gives us flexibility, allowing us to cross-collaborate and adapt, to throw out the org charts and embrace the new horizontal thinking.

This is big talk, but what do I really mean? I'm talking about people organizing *themselves* to solve problems, rather than complaining that the government isn't doing it.

If the armies of Davids who created and used Napster had complained about record companies rather than finding a way to force their hand, people would still be paying for music they don't want—and complaining about it. If Mike Migurski had spent his Christmas break writing letters to the Oakland government rather than creating Crimespotting.org, he'd still be frustrated today.

The old ways we were taught to interact with government—by voting, writing letters, calling our representatives—aren't enough anymore. It's time to break that mold altogether, to embrace a new, technologically aided peer-to-peer way of solving our problems. Let me give you an example of what I mean.

## BYPASSING THE GOVERNMENT

"I was a history teacher in the Bronx for five years," Charles Best told me, "and in my first year of teaching, my colleagues and I would talk about all these ideas we had for projects that would bring the subject matter to life, and resources the kids needed.

"We'd talk about books we wanted them to read, field trips we wanted to take them on, art supplies to do an art project," he told me. "We'd be spending a lot of our own money on basic things like copy paper and pencils and stuff. But these ideas we had for innovations and for resources that would really make a difference wouldn't go beyond the teachers' lunchroom." Why? Because there was no money for such projects in the school's budget and no way to raise money for them. "I figured there were all these people who wanted to improve our public schools, but they were getting more skeptical about giving $100 to a big institution and feeling like their gift was going off into a black hole.

"And I figured if we could enable someone with even one dollar to be a philanthropist and search for classroom projects matching their hometown, their personal values, what they were thinking about the other day, the book they read to their kid last night, and find a classroom project matching that personal passion and then see exactly where their money was going . . . , then the people who wanted to help but were skeptical would be unleashed." This would personalize the whole experience—even more so, Best realized, if he arranged for teachers and kids to write thank-you notes, making donors feel even more invested in the project.

In 2007 Best put his idea into action, launching DonorsChoose.org. It worked exactly as he'd hoped, drawing people in and making them feel connected to the projects they were funding. And it grew like gangbusters: Just three years after launching, in the 2010 school year, DonorsChoose raised $32 million from 350,000 people and helped to fund 70,000 classroom projects.

The lesson? Charles Best didn't spend his time writing letters and complaining to the school board about the lack of money. He saw a problem, created a simple, elegant solution, and just *got it done*. Talk about disintermediation! DonorsChoose cuts right through the clay layer with a message of "Teachers, don't even waste time with your principal—just go online and tell us directly what you want. We'll figure it out—and screw the politics." This is what I mean by peer-to-peer: direct, citizen-driven solutions to problems. The big question is How do we translate that to government?

Stewart Brand gave me a perfect example—a group of military officers bypassing the chain of command to create their own solution to a problem. "There are a lot of really sharp people coming out of the military, and not just officers. . . . They're seriously capable with communication technology and with understanding the combination of hierarchical control and commando collaborative control, which has permeated because of things like PlatoonLeader.com," Brand told me. "PlatoonLeader.com was a problem-solving encouragement network built ad hoc in Iraq." The site was a forum where army officers and noncommissioned officers (NCOs) could exchange information about how to deal with the problems of leading troops in wartime. This was a classic peer-to-peer solution: We need information, so let's get it from each other. No fuss, no muss, no problem. This has to be a good thing, right?

The army, according to Brand, didn't feel that way. "At first, the military said, 'Stand down!'" Brand told me. "But then, some alert officers noticed that their platoon leaders were behaving better when they knew what was going on with the other platoon leaders inside Iraq. And they flipped from resisting it, trying to shut it down, to making it work better." Today, the site—at platoonleader.army.mil— proudly bills itself as a "voluntary community of professionals who love leading soldiers and who are committed to building and leading combat-effective platoons." If a group of dedicated people in the military—the most hierarchical, bureaucratic institution of all—can find a way to bypass authority for the good of their peers, then the rest of us should be able to do the same. We just have to take the initiative.

When you start digging around, you can find plenty of other exam-ples of people finding ways to bypass government:

- In the face of NASA's budget problems, the private company SpaceX is leading the way to the next generation of spaceflight.
- Even as the Solyndra fiasco damaged the government's alternative-energy efforts, the electric-car company Tesla (which has received some government funding) is pushing the boundaries of non-fossil-fuel transport.
- When they felt the government was moving too slowly on genom-ics, Ann Wojcicki and Linda Avey started the genetic testing com-pany 23andMe, pushing the boundaries of genomics further and faster.

"The idea behind 23andMe is let's just bypass the entire system," Wojcicki told me. "Let's empower individuals to do the things they want to do." Yet it's important to realize that you don't have to set up a company, be a billionaire, or create an entire industry to be part of this peer-to-peer revolution. That's the beauty of armies of Davids—even small actions can end up making a huge difference, because of the numbers involved. So how can we maximize the impact of those armies? That's the next piece of the puzzle we have to solve.

## DONORSCHOOSE FOR GOVERNMENT

On your federal tax return, there's a box you can check to direct $3 of your tax payment to the Presidential Election Campaign Fund. The IRS began including this option back in 1973 as a way of paying for election campaigns and party conventions.

Three dollars is a tiny sum—but when tens of millions of people pay it, it becomes a substantial amount. Google has made its fortune by working the magic of large numbers: If you charge a fraction of a penny per page view, that adds up to chump change for most Web sites, but when you have hundreds of millions of page views a day, you make real money.

Why not set up a system whereby people can donate $3 or $5 or however much they want—DonorsChoose-style—to help pay for government projects? What if cash-strapped cities and states in need of funding for things like road repairs or providing free public wi-fi or upgrading their DMV's computer system simply asked citizens to donate specifically toward these projects? Do you think people would give? I do—especially if we could arrange for a tax deduction for the donations.

People want to see results, and filling the potholes in their neighborhood or repairing the sidewalks or fixing the streetlights are all things that improve their lives. Right now, throughout America, people are giving money to publicly funded schools through bake sales, raffles, auctions—anything that will bring in much-needed cash. And that's on top of money the schools already get from the government. There's a clear precedent for this type of giving, and even if only 1 percent of Americans choose to give to such projects, the army-of-Davids effect will ensure that real money will come in to fix real problems.

So let's use the user-friendly, convenient DonorsChoose Web site as a template for use by neighborhoods, towns, and cities to set up their own sites. Like the online toolkits we set up in San Francisco in hopes that other cities could learn from whatever progress and mistakes we've made, let's create toolkits so everyone can easily set up DonorsChoose-style government fund-raising sites.

There's another precedent for this: Through MyBarackObama

.com, thirty-five thousand self-organized communities came together to support Barack Obama's 2008 presidential campaign. Talk about your armies of Davids! This was a campaign by the people, for the people if ever there was one. It's a very American notion—and a very conservative one, in fact. Just do the thing yourself. "We have to get away from the idea that our job as activist citizens is to persuade the government to do something," Tim O'Reilly told me, "as opposed to thinking about how we build mechanisms that'll let us to do things ourselves."

## THE MAN (OR WOMAN) ON THE WHITE HORSE

Early in 2012, I spent a weekend at the Aspen Institute, discussing ideas about leadership and governance. One thing I kept hearing that weekend was, "Revolutions used to have leaders," with the clear implication that this was no longer true. This was the distillation of a question I'd been thinking about for a while: In this new technological age, as ordinary people become increasingly empowered, how important is the traditional notion of leadership? Do we still need—or want—the man or woman on a white horse to swoop in and lead us?

I do believe that we'll always need leaders in politics. As Joe Trippi puts it, "There's a reason we elect a president and a reason we don't have direct democracy. Technology is a great tool for getting people engaged and putting new thinking into government, but there still should be someone saying, 'That's good. That's not.' We elect leaders to make those kinds of decisions."

We used to be a nation of people who looked eagerly to the man on the white horse to save us. From Franklin D. Roosevelt to John

F. Kennedy to Ronald Reagan, we've wanted our presidents to lead so we could follow. But expectations have changed: The days of fireside chats and avuncular Walter Cronkite telling us all what to believe are gone. We have no more common pop-culture references, no common frames of reference in politics. Instead of getting our information from the big three networks and our daily newspaper, we're bombarded on all sides with competing information. We're fragmented in unprecedented ways.

"There will always be the person on the white horse," venture capitalist Mike Moritz told me, "because the promise of the unknown is an easier sell than the familiar." But on the other hand, he says, "The public now is saying, 'Every time I let myself believe in a politician, I get let down.'"

We have to disenthrall ourselves, as Abraham Lincoln used to say, of the notion that politicians and government institutions will solve our problems. The reality is, we have to be prepared to solve our own problems. We will require a different type of government structure to do that, one that makes use of social media, networks, peer-to-peer engagement, and other technological tools. Here's a manifesto that explains exactly what I mean. See if you can guess who wrote it:

> We hope to change how people relate to their governments and social institutions.
>
> We believe building tools to help people share can bring a more honest and transparent dialogue around government that could lead to more direct empowerment of people, more accountability for officials and better solutions to some of the biggest problems of our time.
>
> By giving people the power to share, we are starting to see people make their voices heard on a different scale from what has historically been possible. These voices will increase in number and volume.

They cannot be ignored. Over time, we expect governments will become more responsive to issues and concerns raised directly by all their people rather than through intermediaries controlled by a select few.

Through this process, we believe that leaders will emerge across all countries who are pro-Internet and fight for the rights of their people, including the right to share what they want and the right to access all information that people want to share with them.

So who is this political activist aiming to change the nature of leadership and governance all over the globe? It's Mark Zuckerberg, writing in Facebook's letter to investors prior to its IPO. And the lines dividing the people, the technology, and the governance blur even further.

## THE TWITTER-ENABLED REVOLUTION

For most of human history, revolutions were led by one or more charismatic, powerful people who corralled and led the masses. Yet in the Arab Spring uprisings, more often than not, there was no central authority figure. There was no Martin Luther King Jr., no Nelson Mandela leading the crowds to Tahrir Square. There was only a mass movement, aided by social-networking technology, of people rising up en masse in protest.

This wasn't a Twitter revolution, but Twitter enabled it. It was a fully networked, new-media, leaderless revolution. It signaled that revolutionary change is not personality driven anymore, and that's a profound change. More than ever, what we need is not the man or woman on the white horse, but legions of problem solvers, people who will take problems upon themselves and find solutions to them without waiting for someone in "authority" to show them how.

That's the crux of the matter. It's not that we don't need leaders anymore; it's that those leaders can now come from anywhere, not just the ballot box. They're not one or two people with money or fame or institutionally granted authority. They're a million people posting to their Facebook pages.

I've always loved the idea that "you don't need to *be* somebody to *do* something." The reality is, you simply need to have the conviction of your beliefs. True authority, in this day and age especially, comes less from title and rank than it does from authenticity. Let me explain what I mean.

The leadership guru and author Tom Peters once posed this question: At the peak of their influence, what one thing did Mahatma Gandhi, Martin Luther King Jr., Vaclav Havel, and Nelson Mandela have in common? The answer: jail time. These men were great leaders of their times, and yet none of them started out with even a shred of formal authority. None had been elected or appointed to a position of power or otherwise anointed, but what they lacked in formal authority, they more than made up for in moral authority.

I've always been fascinated by this distinction between moral and formal authority. Formal authority is a twentieth-century model, a relic of the age when power was vested in institutions rather than people. It is power as bestowed through titles rather than power earned through genuine leadership. Moral authority, on the other hand, is granted by the people. It is indifferent to titles, and yet it's invariably more powerful in the end than formal authority.

As technology transforms every facet of our lives, it lays bare this division between moral and formal authority. The people rallying in

Tunisia, the people fighting the repressive Syrian government, the people camping out in New York City's Zuccotti Park, the people creating apps that transform government data into genuine action, the people who take the need for change into their own hands—these are the new leaders on white horses. These are the people who will ultimately change how governments are run. In other words, with the advent of social-networking technology, the leader is us.

# TEN

# Ready, Fire, Aim

WHEN I OPENED MY FIRST PLUMPJACK wine store in San Francisco back in 1992, I didn't really know what I was doing. Since graduating from college three years earlier, my two jobs had been selling shoe orthotics and working at a real estate company. I was twenty-five years old, and it's safe to say that my dreams were bigger than my knowledge about the wine business.

The first couple of years, we struggled to break even. There were wine stores all over the city that gave people what they wanted. What in the world could PlumpJack offer that other stores couldn't? I wanted to make buying wine at PlumpJack a unique experience, but we had very little money to invest in making that happen, so we decided not just to think outside the box, but to act outside it.

Instead of posting *Wine Spectator* reviews, we told people which wines our staff liked. We decorated the interior with affordable wallpaper to fit our Shakespearean theme—Plump Jack is the nickname of John Falstaff, the rotund, comical knight from Shakespeare's plays *Henry the Fourth, Parts One and Two* and *The Merry Wives of Windsor*. We installed a funny little statue of Plump Jack in the store, trying to make it feel unique and inviting. But still the customers weren't coming.

As the adage goes, the two driving forces of life are inspiration and desperation, and that certainly proved true. We'd been inspired to open the store, and now we were desperate to keep it going by any means necessary. In the absence of money to invest, we had to keep innovating.

I decided to go further outside the box. I read that San Francisco's American Conservatory Theater (ACT) company was preparing to stage the play *Cyrano de Bergerac,* so I called them and said, "I know this sounds strange, but would you be willing to come down to my wine store and do a little dress rehearsal there?" It was a long shot, but I figured, why not try? The public rehearsal would help promote ACT, it would bring attention to the store, and it would inject a little fun into people's evening stroll. To sweeten the deal, I offered the actors free wine.

So it was that, one evening not long afterward, people strolling around the Marina District came across a theater troupe—men in tights and floppy hats, women in flowing gowns—reciting couplets in front of our store. This created some buzz and even made it into the paper. And people finally started to notice PlumpJack.

We tried more new things, some that worked and some that didn't. We ran a promotion in which we'd match any other store's price on a particular bottle of wine. We offered a hundred different wines under $10 a bottle. We even offered PlumpJack condoms one Valentine's Day, a promotion I'm not proud of and which to this day makes my father wince. But it got a mention in the *San Francisco Chronicle* at a time when we desperately needed any attention we could get to bring customers into the store.

We also created an award that was dear to my heart: the Failure Award. I used to give the Failure Award out once a month to whichever employee suggested the most fabulous failed idea. I felt strongly then—and still do—that anyone who's not failing isn't trying hard enough. In fact, I'm as proud of some of my failures in business and politics as I am of my successes.

# "I'VE JUST FOUND 10,000 WAYS THAT DON'T WORK"

Failure isn't something to be embarrassed about; it's just proof that you're pushing your limits, trying new things, daring to innovate. As Thomas Edison is alleged to have said about his numerous unsuccessful attempts at creating a light bulb, "I have not failed. I've just found 10,000 ways that don't work." Then, of course, he found a way that did work—and that's all anyone remembers. But Edison never would have gotten there if he had been discouraged rather than energized by his failures.

Our government today is paralyzed by a fear of failure. Taking risks is viewed as reckless, even dangerous, because everyone is so afraid of getting criticized if an initiative fails. But among entrepreneurs, failure is more like a badge of honor. Failing is proof that you weren't afraid to push your limits. In fact, some tech companies won't hire people if they can't point to at least one great failure. We need more of that mind-set in government.

"If somebody starts a company and fails," Roger Ehrenberg says, "then they start another company. If that person was smart and humble and introspective and learned the lessons . . . the odds are that the smart investor would perceive that failure as a positive." As an investor himself, he notes that the founders whose ventures fail often show a great deal of humility and self-awareness afterward. "I think the potential is there, if the language of politics were to change to match the increasing openness that we as general citizens have."

It is too commonplace to blame government ills on public employees, yet the way our civil-service system is currently structured, success is not often defined as achieving results; instead, it's about keeping your head down, putting in the hours, and not breaking the regulatory protocols that have been put into place. Not failing, sadly, is often more important than succeeding. Process and protocol dominate, and outcome is secondary.

In business, of course, the outcome always has to be first—because if you don't make enough money and get customers in the door, your business dies. Anyone who's run even a small business—a pizza parlor, a nail salon, or whatever—knows the feeling of having to innovate to survive. It's in those moments that people come up with some of their best ideas.

If ready, aim, fire is the traditional way to shoot, the business model for PlumpJack was more like ready, fire, aim! We weren't afraid to throw new ideas out there, and ultimately every success came from the ashes of fabulous failures. I had seven years of internalizing that ready, fire, aim mentality before I went into politics. One of my core governing principles—be open to argument and interested in evidence, act on your gut feelings, and sort out the political consequences later—was born out of my experience at PlumpJack.

I'm not here to suggest that government should be run like a business or that politicians should all act like entrepreneurs. However, we do need to take some of the elements of entrepreneurialism—being nimble, networked, innovative, and willing to take risks and make mistakes—and incorporate them into government. Given how fast things are changing and how far behind government is falling, it's the only way we can keep up in our hyperconnected world.

## STEAM, NOT STEM

To be fair, not everyone liked my Failure Award. In fact, when I went into politics and took a less active role at PlumpJack, the company changed the award's name to the more cheery-sounding Magical Moments. I'll grant that rewarding failure isn't the most logical-sounding idea in the world, but I'm fortunate enough not to have an entirely logical mind. That may sound odd, too, but I mean it sincerely.

I don't talk about this often, but I'm dyslexic. Most people associate dyslexia with negative things—difficulty reading, transposing letters, trouble with numbers. I had all those problems. I struggled in school, the guy who never did well in classes, and was always making mistakes.

But the truth is, there's also a tremendous upside to being dyslexic. Yes, I was always making mistakes, but eventually I realized that I just needed to find another way of doing things. As long as I could find a work-around, I could do everything the other kids could do. When you're dyslexic, you have no choice but to learn from your mistakes, because you're pretty much always making mistakes. But many dyslexics are fortunate to also have the skill of three-dimensional problem solving, meaning they're good with hands-on and visual learning, and they often try to solve problems creatively.

So dyslexia gave me the gift of problem solving from a nontraditional perspective. I wasn't afraid to try new things, because that's all I'd ever done. It's the reason I tried to instill unusual business techniques and risk taking at PlumpJack. It's also the reason I moved to allow same-sex marriage in San Francisco in 2004, before any other state or municipality was issuing marriage licenses. It's why I went against the liberal base to start Care Not Cash, why I established universal health care, and why I went out on a limb to create college savings accounts for everyone in San Francisco. I truly believe that if I weren't dyslexic, I wouldn't have done any of those things.

Not everyone who thinks outside the box is dyslexic, of course. That just happened to be my path to thinking differently about the world. But it has been tremendously helpful to me in politics, so I can't help but wish that, in general, we had a greater spirit of risk taking, energy, and creativity in government. Right now, because of the voluminous regulations, the rigidity of the civil-service system, and the clay layers of bureaucracy, whatever creativity there is tends to get crushed.

So how can we encourage more creativity? How can we help people to "think different," as the Apple slogan goes? One way is to go back and start at the beginning, with kids in school, by updating our educational system to focus on STEAM rather than STEM.

In recent years, as the United States has begun to face stiff economic and technological competition from China, South Korea, and other countries, there's been a surge of interest in science, technology, engineering, and mathematics (STEM). It's clear that if we hope to maintain our position as a global leader in innovation, we have to increase the emphasis on these four subjects in our schools.

But STEM alone won't do it. We need to add an A—for arts. Focusing only on the hard sciences isn't enough to stretch the mind and encourage creativity. Take a look at some of our most successful and innovative products: The iPhone is not simply a technological tool; it's a piece of art, a fantastic work of creative design. And the apps that power people's enjoyment of it aren't merely feats of programming; they're feats of imagination. As Albert Einstein famously wrote, "Imagination is more important than knowledge." And imagination is greatly enhanced by exposure to the arts.

The STEAM movement, as befits its focus on creative, out-of-the-box thinking, calls for nothing short of a radical overhaul of our education system. An article on Steam-notStem.com gives some historical perspective on the problem:

> The US education system does what it was designed to do—the problem is that it was formed over 100 years ago in a different time, for a different need, in a different world economy, to satisfy a different lifestyle using the then-available technology.
>
> The US education system has not changed significantly in over 100 years, but the world has.

Sound familiar? It should. The US government is also still functioning much the same way it did a hundred years ago, with the same outdated systems, institutions, and traditions. Remember Mike Lofgren's quote? "Trying to govern a complex society of 310 million people via a museum piece like the Senate is like trying to operate an airline whose fleet consists of Wright Flyers." Well, we're trying to educate 50 million kids in public schools via a museum piece too: our education system. As the article goes on to describe, US schools have retained their industrial-age nature, even as the world has moved on.

> Schools were, and still are, structured like the factories they were developed to serve. They treat education like an assembly line—you move from one task (class) to the next—day in and day out. There is little collaboration or interchange between the work done in one department (course) versus the next. . . .

Our educational system was built to serve a pretechnology, analog society. It's no wonder, then, that innovation in the private and public sectors is at risk of waning—when our educational system rewards test scores and rote memorization rather than creativity and problem solving, our students are learning antiquated skills in a modern world. And that will be a recipe for disaster as the world continues to move toward greater connectivity, innovation, and technological change.

Former secretary of education Richard Riley summed it up perfectly in the same article:

> The jobs in the greatest demand in the future don't yet exist and will require workers to use technologies that have not yet been invented to solve problems that we don't yet even know are problems.

So what can we do? Is there a way we can use technology to modernize our antiquated education system? There is. And a man named Salman Khan is showing us how to do it.

## THE KHAN ACADEMY

Salman Khan was a hedge fund manager in the Boston area when he decided to help out a young cousin in New Orleans who was having trouble with math. It was 2004, and because he was so far away, Khan used Yahoo! Doodle to demonstrate math problems and solutions that his cousin could then watch on her computer over the Internet.

Khan's explanations were clear and simple, and soon his family was requesting more tutorials. In 2006, he began doing videos and posting them on the still relatively new YouTube. He posted them publicly, for anyone to see, and soon he was getting hundreds, then thousands of views. His cousins told him they preferred the YouTube Sal Khan to the real-life Sal Khan, and after giving it some thought, he realized why.

As he explained in a 2011 TED talk, "When you think about it from their point of view, it makes sense. . . . Now they can pause and repeat their cousin, without feeling like they're wasting my time." Not to mention the fact that, when students are trying to learn something, the last thing they need is an adult hovering over them saying, "Do you understand this? Do you get it yet?" Khan's videos allowed the kids to learn at their own pace, to pause and repeat as needed, without having to scramble to take notes even if they weren't really getting what was being taught.

People started leaving comments on Khan's YouTube videos, saying they were finally learning concepts they'd long been struggling with. One parent wrote about an autistic son finally understanding decimals for the first time after watching one of his videos. Being able to go back and rewatch something that didn't make sense the first time ended up being a tremendously helpful tool in learning.

And that's when things really got interesting. As Khan told it in his TED talk, teachers began writing to him, saying, "We've used your videos to flip the classroom. You've given the lectures. So now what I do is, I assign the lectures for homework, and what used to be homework I now have the students doing in the classroom." This may not sound like much of a change, but it's revolutionary. Khan explains why:

> This is the unintuitive thing when you talk about technology in the classroom. By removing the one-size-fits-all lecture from the classroom and letting students have a self-paced lecture at home—and then when you go into the classroom, letting them do work, having the

teachers be able to walk around, having the peers actually interact with each other, these teachers have used technology to humanize the classroom. They took a fundamentally dehumanizing experience—thirty kids with fingers on their lips, not allowed to interact with each other. A teacher, no matter how good, has to give this one-size-fits-all lecture to thirty students, blank faces, slightly antagonistic. And now it's a human experience. Now they're actually interacting with each other.

It seems so simple, so obvious—and yet until Sal Khan came along, no one had realized it: Why have kids do homework at home, where there are no teachers or peers to help them to understand it? Why spend valuable classroom time having kids sit silently, being lectured to—completely wasting those brief periods of time when they're all together and could actually interact meaningfully?

Khan's realization flips the world of teaching on its head. Instead of spending their classroom time lecturing, teachers can instead spend that time actually *teaching*. They can interact with students one-on-one during class, and encourage students to help one another—a kind of peer-to-peer tutoring.

In 2009, Khan quit his job as a hedge fund analyst to start the Khan Academy, which not only puts out tutorial videos but also offers an easy-to-use, color-coded tracking system for teachers so they can easily see which students are having problems with the curriculum. Teachers can then spend time helping the students most in need, pinpointing trouble areas rather than launching blanket lecture explanations that may or may not help those who aren't getting it.

There are other benefits to Khan's video-based learning system. As he noted, "Imagine what that does for the adult learner who's embarrassed." Adults can study in the privacy of their own homes, on their own time, without having to travel to a classroom at a set time every week. Pulling back and looking globally, Khan says, "Imagine what this means to a street kid in Calcutta, who has to help his family during the day and so can't go to school." Khan's system opens up education to anyone with access to the Internet—a number that includes more and more people by the day.

Oh, and one other thing—remember Angry Birds for Democracy? Khan also recognized the incentive value of game mechanics, so he's launched a badge system to get kids excited about learning. Students can earn a whole range of astronomy-themed badges—Meteorite, Moon, Earth, Sun, Black Hole—and there are leaderboards to track who has the most badges. "We have tens of thousands of fifth and sixth graders going in a particular direction depending on what badge you give them," he said.

When Sal Khan started video tutoring for his cousin, he could never have imagined it would one day be used in classrooms. But in the fall of 2010 the school district in Los Altos, California, introduced the Khan Academy videos into two fifth-grade classes and two seventh-grade classes. Since then, the Khan Academy has begun branching into other schools, as well as translating videos into different languages for a global audience.

It's no exaggeration to say that Khan's methods may well transform the way we educate in this country, particularly in light of the fact that legions of others have started following his example with online and blended learning. All because one hedge fund analyst saw a different way of doing things and wasn't afraid to try it. Khan didn't fear failure, and he wasn't afraid of risk. That is the kind of thinking we need to transform education—and government.

# ENTREPRENEUR IN RESIDENCE:
# TODD PARK

Education and government are both stuck in a twentieth-century mind-set, but who is doing in government what Sal Khan is doing in education? Who in government is pushing the envelope, using technology to move beyond business as usual? City governments, as we'll see in chapter 11, are at the forefront of innovation. But there are some very bright lights on the national scene as well—people like Todd Park, the US chief technology officer, who was the CTO of the Department of Health and Human Services when I met with him in the summer of 2011.

I went to Park's office in the HHS building adjacent to the National Mall, not knowing what to expect. It's a little hard to feel inspired walking into that boxy, brown building—it's the kind of place that seems to exude bureaucracy. But when I sat down to talk with Park, his enthusiasm and excitement practically set the room on fire.

Park started out as an entrepreneur. He cofounded two companies, the first when he was just twenty-four. Park had never been in government service and never really contemplated it before he was offered the task of using technology to overhaul the Department of Health and Human Services in 2009. In fact, when he was first approached about the job, he had little idea what HHS even did.

"I was supposed to be an internal change agent," he told me, a broad smile on his face. "An entrepreneur in residence." At first, he was skeptical—why would anyone want to leave the fast-paced, innovative world of start-ups for dry, bureaucratic government service? But he found himself intrigued by the possibilities. "HHS had all this data that was locked away, so I thought, 'What might we be able to do differently?' I fell in love with the opportunity to be helpful."

To Park's amazement, he found the culture and people of HHS incredibly receptive to new entrepreneurial ideas. "The most entrepreneurial time I've ever had has been the last two years," he told me—a statement that sounded like an exaggeration, at least until he started describing to me what he'd been doing over those two years.

"The normal way governments work is, they engage in a waterfall-like process," Park told me. "There's six months of 'strategery,' six months of operations blueprinting, six months of information-technology blueprinting. Then they launch an aircraft carrier that sinks." He laughed. "But you can't split a problem into those three pieces. You have to think across those lines to solve a problem well."

Anyone who's spent time in Washington, D.C., knows that there's a deeply entrenched bureaucratic culture there. So how did Park change it? How did he get people at HHS excited to solve problems in an entrepreneurial way? "The mode of operation that works well is the following," he said. "Whenever I have an idea, the first thing I do is find three to five people here who had the idea a long time ago and know how to make it work. Then I recruit them to join a 'virtual start-up' that acts, quacks, and moves like a Silicon Valley start-up, running at Silicon Valley speed—experimenting and learning on the fly, engaging customers to guide the work, to understand what the problem really is. We're able to get big things done in really short time frames. The waterfall method doesn't work. Small, interdisciplinary, agile teams, thinking like a single collective mind, engaging customers as soon as possible with a minimum viable product—that's what works."

But could Park really instigate that much change that quickly in an entrenched D.C. bureaucracy? Historically, we're all about input—how much are we spending on this program? How many people are on staff?—rather than the output of, is this program working? Is it changing people's lives for the better? In government, we're excessively focused on protocols and rules rather than people.

In Park's view, people are the most important element. "The secret [to HHS's success] is the people on those teams. The core of what I've done is just recruit people into teams to do things they've always wanted to do," he told me. "Many of the most talented entrepreneurs I've ever met work at HHS. You could put them in a room with the best entrepreneurs I've worked with in the private sector and you couldn't tell the difference. They're brash, they're mission driven, they're highly gifted change agents. The key is finding those people and weaponizing them."

## "IT'S ALREADY OUT OF CONTROL!"

OK, that's a lot of big talk, but what specifically had HHS done during Park's tenure? When I asked him that question, he began talking and didn't stop for a good half hour. With growing excitement, he told me about all these new programs:

- **A Microsoft Bing app that provides real data on hospital quality.** When you search for a hospital using the Bing search engine, you don't get just addresses. You get ratings of all the nearby facilities—patient satisfaction figures versus the national average, with links to even more information on hospital quality. Prior to Park's tenure, all those invaluable data were just sitting in obscure government servers, used by many fewer people than needed the information.

- **Community Health Status Indicators,** a public dashboard that shows you, at a glance, how healthy your community is. What percentage of residents smoke? What is the leading cause of death? How physically active are people in your community? How does your community compare to others in your city? The site stimulates discussion and even competition, as communities try to improve their health indicators.

- **Food Oasis,** a new app, created in a matter of hours by a Pittsburgh hackathon team, to help people in low-income areas. The "food desert" phenomenon refers to areas where people don't have access to affordable healthy food. The Food Oasis app, Park told me, is "a brilliant mash-up of texting and farmers' markets. You text to a number and say, 'I need five tomatoes.' Because there's no physical infrastructure, and the demand is known in advance, the cost of food drops." Farmers' markets increase sales, people get healthy food, costs drop. Everyone wins.

- **Community Clash,** a card game app that compares health data for various cities. Players are dealt five cards relating to a particular city, showing health factors like smoking, obesity, drug use. They swap out cards to improve their scores, trying to outdo other cities. A kind of Angry Birds for Democracy, Community Clash offers a way for people to learn and engage with government data while having a lot of fun doing it.

- **The Network of Care for Healthy Communities,** a Web portal that offers a full directory of health services, twenty thousand health-related links, and a legislative section with information on every single bill that relates to health. Once again, a fabulous new tool is created from data that for years simply languished in PDFs and on hard drives.

- **Asthmapolis**—a fantastically simple, sensible way to help
  asthma sufferers. An inhaler is fitted with a GPS tracking device,
  so that every time the person suffers the effects of asthma and has
  to inhale, the location is automatically noted. In a test, users of this
  device were able to cut their rate of uncontrolled asthma in half—
  they'd see patterns of what areas and activities were causing their
  asthmatic symptoms to spike and learn to avoid them.

"The best part of all of this," Park told me, "was that HHS didn't have
to do any of it. We just took the data, made it available and machine-
readable, and promoted it to innovators." And those innovators ran
with it. "If you look at the innovations we have coming in, no one
organization—no ten organizations!—could have dreamed this stuff
up," Park said.

Park told me about Joy's law, the maxim named for Bill Joy, the
cofounder of Sun Microsystems: "No matter who you are, most of the
smartest people work for someone else." "A lot of enthusiasm got generated by that," Park told me. "Internally, HHS people said, 'Wow! If
we make our data liquid and open, other people will turn it into apps
or services we wouldn't have thought of, let alone built. . . . Let's just
have all the other smart people in the world leverage our data to develop
and deploy new products and services that help improve health.'" That's
real innovation—throwing the doors open so that people can create
useful, fun stuff that improves lives. That's the kind of risk taking and
entrepreneurial thought that can vastly improve our governance.

"One of the best things about where we are," Park told me, "is
that things are already out of control! Our object was for innovation
leveraging our data to get out of control as fast as possible, and it did."
For most people—especially those in government—getting "out of

control" is just about the scariest thing imaginable. For Todd Park, it's thrilling. "We couldn't be happier about that," he said.

The other people at HHS seemed pretty thrilled, too. When the secretary of HHS, Kathleen Sebelius, issued an executive order asking all the department's agencies to publish a "data liberation plan" every six months, detailing what data they've made accessible and what new data they planned to release, the response from the trenches was not what you'd expect. Honestly, I'd have thought people would fight back and complain about having to put all that information out there, but according to Park, the response at HHS was the opposite. "As opposed to people thinking of it as a root canal–type compliance exercise, they got really passionate about it," Park said. "Suddenly they were telling us about all this data we didn't even know we had! It all goes back to the point that it's not about someone like me arriving from the outside, landing like an alien, and telling people what to do. It's about finding these people who know more than you do, and unleashing them to do the things they've been wanting to do."

## INNOVATION VERSUS STATUS QUO

As I was talking with Todd Park, he kept mentioning *The Lean Startup* author Eric Ries, whose theories on entrepreneurial and innovative thinking impressed Park so much that he decided to meet with him. "Talking to Eric was like talking to someone who had X-rayed my body to see all of my broken bones, from all the lessons I'd learned the hard way as an entrepreneur, and then had codified how to help others learn those same lessons—minus the bone breaking," Park told me.

A couple of months later, Ries and I met in San Francisco, and he walked me through his thoughts on government, bureaucracy, and innovation. "The deep problem is really not about technology or government per se," Ries told me. "It's about developing new management tools, particularly with the level of uncertainty we're trying to cope with in our society. This is stressful, but it's also a really interesting opportunity. And it's something that, as an opportunity, was not faced by people even fifty years ago."

As Ries describes it, society was for many years focused on how to get enough stuff—food, clothing, shelter—for people to survive. Over time, he says, "we as a society cracked that basic problem." We can build, grow, harvest, and distribute goods more efficiently than ever before. So now we need to shift our focus away from that more-or-less solved problem, to focus on innovating into the future.

"There's a holy war going on between the forces of status quo and the forces of innovation. . . . We pay managers to defend the status quo and keep it from breaking. And they get in big trouble if they screw up. And there's not really much payoff for them if they adapt," he said, echoing the point about government that I'd heard from so many others: that government isn't interested in *solving* problems so much as *managing* them.

For years, the goal of our government bureaucracy has been to keep things going the same way they've always gone, to maintain the status quo. But today, in a world where new technology and peer-to-peer networking are heralding the death of hierarchy—in business, in society, and soon enough in government—Reis, like Park, argues that putting more power in the hands of the people is the way forward.

"The problem is never with the end employees," Ries told me. "I could ask any government employee, 'Have you got five minutes? Can you tell me some ways your agency could help citizens better?' You can't shut them up!" So just as Park did with his HHS employees, managers have to let people take a real, active role in how their department or government agency is run. Managers have to let people take ownership far more than they do now. "The employee suggestion box is the classic example," Ries said. "There might as well be a shredder on the other side."

Some private-sector companies have figured out better ways to engage their employees. "At Toyota, they spend a lot of time developing their incentives and systems," Ries said. "You have an idea for how to make something better, you tell your manager, and he or she has a discretionary budget to implement the suggestion. . . . As an employee, you have a chance to have your idea seen at the highest levels of the company." And ideas, he said, are labeled with the innovator's name: "Inside the company, they don't call it the Camry. It's so-and-so's car. I presume that if I talked to the people who work at a Toyota plant and said, 'How would you get an idea implemented?' they'd know. They'd at least know the first step. And they would believe it would have a chance. For most people who work at any other large organizations"— including government—"they look at me funny. It's, like, such a weird question. 'It's not even relevant. I don't know. Maybe go lobby somebody?'"

This observation in particular really struck me. If you have a fantastic idea for improving a government service, how do you get it implemented? How do good ideas make it through the clay layer of bureaucracy? At Todd Park's HHS, employees were able for the first time to get their ideas heard, and the results were spectacular. We need to open up those communication lines in other government agencies too. Otherwise we're just wasting the skills and knowledge of the very people who have the best ideas.


## THE UPSIDE OF HAVING NO MONEY

Due to the recent economic downturn, ballooning deficits, and ongoing concerns over the future of Social Security and Medicare, it's clear that austerity is the new norm. We can't just cut and tax our way out of problems, we still have to solve them. How? We have to innovate and invent our way out.

This might sound perverse, but in some ways I like not having money, as it forces a new way of thinking about things. At PlumpJack, when we couldn't afford a desk, we just put an old door on top of four wine cases, a solution that was just as functional and also had more charm. When San Francisco's Recreation and Parks Department was struggling with underused facilities that were falling into disrepair, we started a program called Rec Connect, matching nonprofits and their needs to city recreation centers. Once those nonprofits started hosting activities and taking an interest in the facilities, they became vibrant community hubs. People began taking care of the rec centers and clubhouses rather than waiting for government to do it. Everybody won.

The fascinating thing is that if we'd had enough money to care for the facilities in the first place, none of this wonderful community involvement would have happened. We were forced to innovate, and the innovated solution turned out to be much better than simply throwing money at the problem.

Innovation isn't just about new technology; it's also about using existing technology in an innovative way. Project Homeless Connect was the perfect example: It combined data with civic engagement to create a new way of treating homeless people's problems. We brought in dentists, opticians, mental-health professionals, lawyers, wheelchair repair people, employment counselors—all of them under one roof to give vital services to homeless people. Government doesn't have to provide an expensive, stand-alone service; it just has to connect people and build partnerships.

The more we get people engaged, the less money we have to spend on getting things done. When Dustin Haisler was looking to engage the citizens of Manor, Texas, for as little money as possible, he started posting QR codes all over the city. Initial cost? "Four hundred dollars," he said. "Just the cost of the paper and ink." In the twenty-first century, innovation plus technology is the only way to overcome our deficits and provide for all our citizens.

# ELEVEN

# The Postpartisan Age

IF THERE'S ONE BRIGHT SPOT IN politics today, one place where innovation is happening and people are taking at least some part in governance, it's in our cities. Unlike state and national governments, city governments know they must produce results or risk losing residents. The reason? People will happily move to a new town if they think they'll be better off. If people don't like how the federal government operates, leaving the country isn't usually a realistic option, but if a city begins to fall apart and civic leaders can't stem the bleeding, people will leave. Just ask Detroit.

There's competition among cities, the kind of competition that keeps them innovating, because people can and do compare services in their town to those in other towns. How many times have you had a conversation with a friend, coworker, or relative, comparing the state of the roads on your commute or swapping stories about how often your garbage gets picked up? People talk about this stuff all the time, so city officials know their job is simple: Take care of the residents' needs.

When mayors get together, they tend to freely exchange information about how to improve their cities. They share everything. "You got private financing for a new park? How did you do that?" "Here's how we made room for bicycle lanes downtown." "Oh, we had that problem too. Let me tell you how we fixed it." Cities may be in competition with one another, but mayors seem more than happy to cooperate.

That's because all mayors are in the same business—the "reduce traffic, snowplow the streets fast, fix broken stoplights" business. Bad traffic is high on every city's complaint list, so all mayors spend time and money trying to crack that nut. If everyone compared notes and shared success stories, we could go a long way toward alleviating that vexing problem. And with today's technology, sharing that information is easier than ever—if we'll just step up and do it.

Why not create a national site for the kind of policy toolkits we put online when I was mayor of San Francisco? We could launch a one-stop destination for innovation, ideas, and resources to better our cities, with open conversation threads to discuss what works and what doesn't. We could call it CityChat, a place where not only city officials, but all people wanting to improve their cities can meet and talk and learn. We have the technology to do this. What are we waiting for?

How about replicating that Facebook-for-spooks site, A-Space, as a kind of Facebook for cities? Why not create a specialized social-networking site—call it C-Space—for mayors, administrators, programmers, and others who want to improve city life? After all, if mayors are so eager and willing to share information when they meet at conferences, shouldn't they be able to share it without having to travel hundreds of miles just to be in the same room? Isn't that what the promise of technology is all about?

## IF MAYORS RULED THE WORLD

If cities are laboratories of innovation, our states are laboratories of democracy. State government is far more political and partisan than city government. In state elections, voters really care whether they elect a Republican or Democrat. But in cities, they just want the pragmatist, the woman or man who'll be able to *get stuff done*. After all, there's no Democratic or Republican way to remove graffiti.

Cities are crucial for other reasons, too. The economic output of this country and increasingly the world originates in the metro regions. We've entered the era of metro versus metro, when it's not America competing with China, but rather Boston Area biotech companies competing with tech clusters in Shanghai. For the first time in history, more people worldwide now live in cities than in rural areas—and that has changed the face of life and business.

Professor Benjamin Barber, a political theorist and author of the 1996 bestseller *Jihad vs. McWorld,* believes strongly that cities are the future. His new book, *If Mayors Ruled the World,* makes the case that mayors essentially act as cross-border problem solvers. Barber talked about this idea in a series of speeches he gave throughout the country in 2012:

> The paramount aims of city dwellers concern collecting garbage and collecting art rather than collecting votes or collecting foreign allies, the supply of water rather than the supply of arms, promoting cooperation rather than promoting exceptionalism, fostering education and culture rather than fostering national defense and patriotism. . . .
>
> Cities can make themselves global guarantors of social justice and equality against the depredations of fractious states. And then can become, as the *polis* [Greek city-state] once was, new incubators of democracy, this time in a global form.

Wim Elfrink, who spent years building Smart+Connected Communities in India as part of a Cisco Systems project, echoes Barber's view.

"I strongly believe in cities as the center of innovation," Elfrink told me. To drive home his point, he noted that "the absolute gross domestic product of New York City is the same as the GDP of India."

Cities are the new economic engines. They're also places where partisan politics must take a backseat to real postpartisan innovation and risk taking. They are the places where the vast, seemingly intractable problems of our age will begin to be solved.

Take climate change, for example. Although it is clearly a global problem, the reality is climate change results from the sum total of local consumption and local pollution. We don't pollute as one monolithic nation; each region has its own factories, traffic, and regulations. So we have to deal with local consumption and pollution at their source: in cities and municipalities. Mayors and city administrators must lead the way in terms of climate resolutions, and they have to communicate to each other the best practices for doing so. Only then can we begin to solve the problem.

As Stewart Brand told me, "Mayors have more power than anybody. And mayors are closer to a genuine responsive feedback system than anybody, because the stuff the mayor does plays out in a matter of months. You get to see if it works, make adjustments, learn from it, cite actual behavior. With state and federal, there are so many delays that the sausage isn't recognizable." But mayors can be instantly responsive to constituents—and this is truer than ever in the age of technology.

Newark mayor Cory Booker offers the perfect example of this. When he launched his Twitter feed, he created a mechanism to respond instantly to people's needs. On December 31, 2010, a constituent with the Twitter handle @BigSixxRaven tweeted the mayor, asking him to send someone to shovel snow from her sixty-five-year-old father's driveway. Mayor Booker tweeted back, "Please @BigSixxRaven don't worry about ur dad. Just talked 2 him & I'll get 2 his driveway by noon. I've got salt, shovels & great volunteers."

Not surprisingly, Booker's constituents—and the media—went crazy. The mayor was listening to them! He was a hero! The simple act of making himself available and showing that he was responsive to their concerns brought Mayor Booker closer to his Newark citizens than any press release or planned public appearance ever could have.

This is the kind of power that can be unleashed by the simple equation of city government + superconnective technologies. "Cities have been doing for seven thousand years what cell phones are doing now," says Stewart Brand. "Now imagine that the things we've come to understand about how cities work and are trying to work better could be applied directly to state, federal, global affairs. . . ." That's when we'll have truly harnessed the power of technology for good.

## BRINGING BACK THE COMMONWEALTH

In October 2011, the New America Foundation released *Hear Us Now? A California Survey of Digital Technology's Role in Civic Engagement and Local Government*, a report about technology and civic innovation. The introduction offered an optimistic view of the future:

> Hidden in all the bad news about California's troubles is this delightful paradox: Californians, while living in a state that experts say is ungovernable, have within their reach new tools that give them greater power to govern themselves than ever before.

Technology is the reason. Often with little public notice or scrutiny, most of California's [ . . . ] local governments are experimenting with technologies to engage the public and improve services. The sophistication of this use of digital technologies for citizen interaction—referred to as eGovernment, digital government, or Government 2.0—varies. The benefits are wide-ranging.

The report went on to detail a number of innovative city- and county-based initiatives, such as:

- A text-messaging network in San Ramon Valley that allows people to quickly contact a CPR-certified citizen in the vicinity if someone suffers cardiac arrest.
- An online sign-up to have the Santa Clarita city police check your home while you're away on vacation.
- A Pebble Beach Community Services database of people who need special assistance in the event of an emergency evacuation.
- Digital channels that provide farmers in Riverside County with up-to-the-minute weather data to help them minimize irrigation and maximize their crop yields.

And this is only the beginning. Using new technologies in these ways, local governments can transform the citizen-government relationship, which has been weakened by the transience of populations, lack of resources, partisanship, and other vagaries of the modern civic experience.

Perhaps the most interesting point of all: It is only through our futuristic new twenty-first-century technology that we can hope to recapture the age-old notion of commonwealth—meaning a public good or welfare that exists among a community of people. For centuries, the idea of commonwealth held people together during wars, famine, and political upheaval. Commonwealth was the foundation of society, the glue that held communities together and drove public life. It's a notion that began to disappear in twentieth-century America, as urbanization and greater mobility led to the fracturing of community life. But now it can be resurrected through technology.

While I was in Washington, D.C., doing interviews for this book, I was surprised at how many people talked about this notion of commonwealth. There's a pervasive sense of trying to bring back that feeling of community, public good, and collective welfare that drove civilization for so long. This is democracy going back to its roots, back to the local level, where change occurs.

This was Tocqueville's ideal, the New England townships where civic engagement and public education took place, where people gathered around to get information and interact. "The village or township is the only association which is so perfectly natural that, wherever a number of men are collected, it seems to constitute itself," Tocqueville wrote. "The town . . . exists in all nations, whatever their laws and customs may be."

Technology can help us recapture the spirit of these townships; it can help us recapture that connectedness we've lost over the last few decades. A line by the social epidemiologist Richard Wilkinson seems to sum up the feeling: "If Americans want to live the American dream, they should go to Denmark." America has become so big, diverse, urbanized, economically stratified, and politically partisan that it's having a hard time maintaining the notion of commonwealth. But the notion of Citizenville, at its heart, is really just an updated version of the township—a place where residents gather to take care of their societal needs. A place where people nourish and strengthen the commonwealth.

"The way that you try to counteract the perils of scale is by going local, and through local empowerment," Roger Ehrenberg told me. "I'm talking about people and politicians being responsible and caring about their area." And the way to do that? "Social networks are bringing people together, getting them to open up. Translate that into offline activity. You see it in things like Meetups, the melding of online and offline. It is real. But then how do you bring that to government?"

Ehrenberg went on to answer his own question. "It takes a holistic approach. Let's say someone builds a great neighborhood-collaboration app"—something like Citizenville, for example—"but if the cities don't support it, and they don't listen, who cares? It doesn't do anything. . . . It's not going to have the fundamental effect of changing the quality of life in a city, much less the country. It can't be, well, the government just throws money at it. We need ideas from below."

In other words, we need contests, X Prizes, politically oriented social-networking sites, and government apps stores—all the things in the private sector that have been proven to generate excitement, creativity, and great innovation from ordinary people. These are the ways we can reignite the public's passion for civic engagement.

## THE END OF BOUNDARIES

Everything I've written about in this book comes down to a simple premise: Technology puts power in the hands of the people—if only we let it. And given the fact that our governments—local, state, federal—are perennially short of money and mired in bureaucracy, this transfer of power is clearly the key to democratizing our voices, bringing our nineteenth-century government into the twenty-first century.

But here's the fascinating thing: It's not that technology strengthens government. Instead, technology changes the very nature of government—from a top-down entity to a bottom-up one. From one-way hierarchy to two-way democracy. From the vending machine to the cloud. This is the promise of Citizenville: The democratizing influence of the cloud leads to a stronger, more stable commonwealth.

That transformation will have another effect, too: It will blur the lines between federal, state, and local divisions. Just as cities have become laboratories for innovation, these peoplecentric technologies have become the vanguard of new forms of governance. Citizen engagement in the twenty-first century won't be about congressional and presidential elections; it will be about personal involvement at the most local levels, a collective community empowerment that then works its way up to the highest levels of governance. It will be about individuals organizing themselves, taking care of their communities, and, when necessary, forcing government to change its ways to address their needs. None of us is an expert in everything; if government can encourage collective expertise and the democratization of voices, we'll all be better off.

Monolithic institutions are a thing of the past. In the private sector today, talent often resides outside the boundaries of companies and businesses, as we've seen with iPhone apps and open-source software projects. In every aspect of American life—the media, entertainment, music, you name it—the days when a handful of entities controlled the public's attention are over.

Mitch Kapor, founder of Lotus Development and cofounder of the Electronic Frontier Foundation, told me, "If you can free people from being held down or oppressed by systems, whether public or private, . . . people can choose to make things that suit themselves. We used to live in a world with three TV networks. Now we live in a world where there are a hundred million YouTube videos of dogs on roller skates." We have entered the era of choice, and although we as a society may not need a hundred million videos of roller-skating dogs, we do need the ability for people to create and distribute information freely.

The silos that used to define public life are crumbling, replaced by far-reaching community networks. It's no wonder our big, traditional government institutions are failing. The ideas behind them are anathema to a whole new generation of Americans.

There's a lot of talk these days about public-private partnerships, those joint ventures between businesses and government agencies that are intended to lower the costs and raise the efficiency of civic projects. This has been a hot topic in the age of austerity, but public-private partnerships are too limited. What we're missing out on, and what the new age of networking will engender, is public-public partnerships: cities collaborating with cities, neighborhoods collaborating with neighborhoods. It's San Jose partnering with San Francisco to create the first electric-battery switching stations for electric taxicabs. It's a public-school district collaborating with a city to create a comprehensive arts education curriculum for students. It's public universities collaborating with cities to guarantee four-year college education for students. It's public schools making a deal with public-health nurses so that kids have proper health care through on-site wellness centers.

Public-public partnerships are all about networking, coordinating resources, and leveraging existing money. They're about doing more with less, aided by technology. In California, we have 476 cities, 58 counties, and hundreds of departments and agencies within those areas. How much good could we do if all those entities shared their resources and knowledge? And how easy would it be to do that, in the new age of networking? It all comes down to the same thing: giving power to the people. The ultimate public-public partnership, the final frontier of this new paradigm, is people sharing with people, building a new form of governance from the ground up.

This isn't an ideological battle, and it's not the province of either Democrats or Republicans. It's the ideology of efficiency. Arianna Huffington told me, "This is not a question of Drudge or *HuffPost* or Fox. There's an enormous amount of thinking around that, the fact that we tend to look at what is happening in terms of left versus right, without new thinking on the major problems we're facing." It's time to get past that kind of partisan mind-set.

"If you're successful in building these social media ties, there will be less partisanship," Matt Lira, the tech guru for Majority Leader Eric Cantor, said in our interview. And it's inevitable that those social media ties will continue to grow. "In the future, everything will become insanely more social, to a degree we can't even fully conceptualize," he told me. "We'll have interactive TV shows, real-time feedback. Facebook is doing presidential debates and thinking about having real-time polls, where the candidate answers a question and the follow-up is 'Well, eighty percent of people we just polled don't like your answer.'" This kind of technology empowers not the Democrats, not the Republicans, not the politicians at all, in fact. It empowers the people.

And that's the final, most important point. Using technology to connect Americans to their government is not a political cause. It's a *moral* cause. As a politician, I try to keep these questions in mind: Who do we really represent? And what are we really trying to achieve? Serving the people means trying to create a just society—a society where people's views are represented and their needs fulfilled. Right now, our system for doing that is broken. Fixing it—through the use of these new technologies—is bigger than politics and partisanship. It's a matter of justice.

In a letter written from jail in Birmingham, Alabama, Dr. Martin Luther King Jr. wrote, "We are caught in an inescapable web of mutuality, tied in a single garment of destiny. Whatever affects one directly affects us all indirectly." We've lost that sense of mutuality in recent years. Let's empower people to give voice to their surroundings and their realities, to multiply their voices in public. Let's make Citizenville a reality.

# ACKNOWLEDGMENTS

Many people were instrumental in making *Citizenville* a reality. I had the joy and delight of working and collaborating with Lisa Dickey—I could not have asked for a better partner throughout this project. My agent, Elyse Cheney, has been terrific. She kept with me over a number of years as I developed the ideas contained here. And I am grateful to my editor, Ann Godoff, for believing in this book.

On the policy front, I want to thank Tim O'Reilly and Jen Pahlka for their example and inspiration—in many ways, their work was the inspiration for this book. I also had the good fortune to work with Yashar Hedayat, who helped me identify key leaders in the field of technology and governance and helped arrange difficult to get interviews.

Peter Ragone relentlessly encouraged me to take on this project and never let up until the final page. He was instrumental in not only finishing, but beginning the book. I deeply appreciate his support. I would also like to thank my chief of staff, Chris Garland, and Jason Kinney.

To my extraordinary wife, Jen, and my two beautiful children, Montana and Hunter—I love you more than words could possibly express.

Thank you, Jen, for your wisdom, sense of purpose, and support through this project. You have been a terrific ally and a wonderful adviser throughout. To my kids, whom I hope will one day read this book—the "digital natives" who will grow up in a world I could only have dreamed of—I hope you will be proud of it.

Thanks also to the many people who agreed to share their thoughts on technology, politics, and our future—I learned a tremendous amount from each of you, and I deeply appreciate your help:

Shawn Allen, Warren Beatty, Marc Benioff, Charles Best, Cory Booker, Stewart Brand, Sergey Brin, Aneesh Chopra, Bill Clinton, George Clooney, Peter Diamandis, Mark Drapeau, Roger Ehrenberg, Wim Elfrink, Greg Ferenstein, Ted Gaebler, David Gavigan, Kevin Gessay, Al Gore, Dustin Haisler, Peter Hirshberg, Arianna Huffington, Chris Hughes, Mitch Kapor, Guy Kawasaki, Salman Khan, Maria Teresa Kumar, Vivek Kundra, Matt Lira, Mike Migurski, Ellen Miller, Mike Moritz, Craig Newmark, Edward Norton, Tim O'Reilly, Jen Pahlka, Todd Park, Tiago Peixoto, Tom Peters, Brian Purchia, Dylan Ratigan, Eric Reis, Shauna Robertson, Simon Rosenberg, Alec Ross, Sheryl Sandberg, Elliot Schrage, Peter Schwartz, Clay Shirky, Rachel Sterne, Jeremy Stoppelman, Kara Swisher, Don Tapscott, Joe Trippi, Steven VanRoekel, Chris Vein, Evan Williams, and Anne Wojcicki.

My thanks to all government workers whose work directly and indirectly impacts all our lives each and every day. And to elected officials of all stripes—a heartfelt thank-you for stepping up to serve the public. Thank you for not sitting on the sidelines and for being willing to suffer the slings and arrows so often associated with public service.

And finally, thank you to the people of San Francisco and my home state of California for giving me the privilege of a lifetime to serve as county supervisor, mayor, and now lieutenant governor. I am grateful to you for allowing me to test ideas, periodically shake up the status quo, make the occasional mistake, and fulfill my passion for public service.

# INDEX